Playing **Politics**

The Nightmare Continu

Michael Laver has been playing ga............ ....e.
He now finds it impossible to tell what is a game and what
is the 'real' world but has so far been able to avoid being
mown down by a real twenty-ton truck, find time to write
books on various aspects of politics, and thereby appear to
be a political scientist. The most recent of his books are
Making and Breaking Governments (1996, with Ken Shepsle),
and *Private Desires, Political Action* (1997). During the
daylight hours, he assumes the role of Professor of Political
Science at Trinity College Dublin.

Playing **Politics**
The Nightmare Continues

MICHAEL LAVER

Oxford   New York

OXFORD UNIVERSITY PRESS

1997

Oxford University Press, Great Clarendon Street, Oxford OX2 6DP

Oxford New York

Athens Auckland Bangkok Bogota Bombay Buenos Aires
Calcutta Cape Town Dar es Salaam Delhi Florence Hong Kong
Istanbul Karachi Kuala Lumpur Madras Madrid Melbourne
Mexico City Nairobi Paris Singapore Taipei Tokyo Toronto Warsaw
and associated companies in
Berlin Ibadan

Oxford is a trade mark of Oxford University Press

British Library Cataloguing in Publication Data
Data available

Library of Congress Cataloging in Publication Data
ISBN 0–19–285321–X (Pbk.)

10 9 8 7 6 5 4 3 2 1

Typeset by Best-set Typesetter Ltd., Hong Kong
Printed and bound in Great Britain by
Biddles Ltd., Guildford and King's Lynn

Preface

This is not the sort of book that merits a long and tedious Preface. There really are only a very few things that need to be said before we roll up our sleeves and get on with the important business of playing politics.

It is now nearly twenty years since I produced my first book of political games, *Playing Politics*, which was published by Penguin Books in 1979. An awful lot has changed since then. Perhaps the most important change is that some people, at least, no longer regard playing political games as a peculiar or eccentric thing to do, but can see a point in it all. In a way this is a shame, since it's always nice to find peculiar or eccentric ways of doing things. But, on balance, it's marvellous, since many are now much more open to the idea that games can indeed teach us important things about how human beings interact with one another.

So the time seems ripe for a second book of games. This sits somewhere in between a second edition of the first book and a completely new book in its own right—hence the subtitle. Early versions of several of the games that follow were in the original version of *Playing Politics*, but each of these games has been extensively developed and modified as a result of lessons learned over another twenty years of playing them. There are also several completely new games, including a new class of political games—these are 'political' versions of familiar non-political games, such as poker, darts, and soccer. Above all, however, thanks largely to the activities of many student game-players over the years, the big change is that there are now much more lively and fast-paced ways of running the games. This is most obvious in the use of soundtracks that alternate rock music and silence to mark the passing of political day and political night, but the use of lighting, costumes, and many other bits and pieces besides all mean, I hope, that each of the games is definitely more fun to play.

I'll say no more about the games here since, as any game-player knows, the first rule of gaming is that the way to find out about any game is to play it, not to read about it.

What remains is to thank many people, so many, in fact, that it's not fair to single any of them out for special mention, although some very definitely deserve it. I hope that they know who they are anyway. The book *certainly* would not have been possible without the enthusiasm, ingenuity, and warmth, the wonderful deviousness and the simple down-home goodwill, of so many people who have played these games with me over the years. These have included groups, listed in chronological order as far as I can remember them, at the University of Essex, Queen's University Belfast, Liverpool University, the University of Texas at Austin, University College Galway, Harvard University, Trinity College Dublin, and the University of Nijmegen. For three years, students in one of my courses at Trinity not only played the games with good humour and tolerance, but devised games of their own that were often much better than mine, and were thus an unceasing source of inspiration. The final run-though of a number of the games in this book was at the University of Turku, at which a kind and enthusiastic group of Finnish students found a place in their schedule for a visiting madman.

As the manuscript neared completion, several people read it and made (mostly) polite suggestions about how to improve it. As a result of their efforts, the end-product is a little less wild but a lot more reader-friendly, so readers, as well as I, should thank them too.

MICHAEL LAVER

Dalkey, September 1996

Contents

1 Introduction

This is a book of games and a book about politics. I do hope the games are fun to play and I do hope that they can be enjoyed by people who don't care at all about politics. The games do, however, have a serious purpose; each is an attempt to capture one of the many intriguing puzzles that run through political life.

Politics is not a game, of course; it's a serious business. Nevertheless, one important aspect of politics is like a game. What actually happens is usually the result of calculated and calculating interaction between self-seeking political actors, be they private individuals, politicians, political parties, pressure groups, national governments, or even whole alliances of countries. Calculated and calculating interaction is what games are all about.

The purpose of this book is to distil some of the essence of these real political interactions and to present them as simple games that anyone can play. The reason for doing this is not just so that everyone can have fun and not at all to suggest that politics is a trivial process. Everyone really ought to have fun and politics may indeed seem trivial to certain world-weary eyes, but I do hope that exploring the simplified dilemmas that follow will give people at least some sort of a feel for the fascinating complexity of real-world politics.

Before getting down to business I should come clean about my own political persuasions. I am a practising political scientist. As if that was not bad enough I am, sad to say, also something of a cynic when it comes to politics and have to confess that some of this cynicism may sometimes carry through into the games in this book. These games probably do present politics as a rather cynical process and politicians as rather cynical people. This is not quite as depressing as it might seem at first sight, however, since the book is not about any of the great issues of politics. Rather, it is about the nitty-gritty of getting your own way, *whatever that might be*.

Some of the games give players policy preferences that they simply cannot change—sensitive readers can call these ideals if it makes them feel better. However, all of the games are about means rather than ends. The cut and thrust that runs through each of them is as likely in the workplace, in a sports club or in a commune as it is in a modern Western democracy or an old-fashioned dictatorship. The ends that people strive towards, of course, may be very different in each setting; but the means that people use to achieve these ends can be uncannily similar. Even the most fervent of idealists, if they are to be effective in this imperfect world we all live in, must get their hands dirty from time to time in pursuit of their lofty ideals. If there are any idealists who haven't already thrown this book on to the bonfire, therefore, I humbly suggest to them that the games which follow may teach them *something*, at least, about how to get their hands dirty to maximum effect.

WHAT YOU NEED TO PLAY POLITICS

People

You need people to play politics. Ideally these should be enemies since this makes winning so much more fun. It also means you have less to lose, since some of the players will end up hating each other before the games are over. If you can't find a group of enemies to play with, a group of friends will just have to do. Or you may be lucky enough to have control over a captive audience. Teachers, for example, often have captive groups of students at their mercy for apparently interminable periods of time, and can subject these to many different types of cruel and unusual punishment. For a change they could try games.

If the people at your disposal don't like games that's OK. Just force them to play anyway, using whatever means of persuasion or coercion you have at your disposal. Either they'll still hate games at the end of it all, in which case nothing in the least will have been lost; or they'll have learned to love games in the meantime, in which case a very great deal will have been gained. You can't lose. And believe me, it's great fun watching those grumpy humanoids who like to sit and sneer on the sidelines, and who are really just worried about looking like idiots, stop combing their hair and start hopping up and down in their seats as the deals start to roll. Sooner rather than later, the urge to get in on the action becomes impossible to resist and those who once sneered throw dignity to the winds as they roll up their sleeves and get down to the business of winning. So make them do it for their own good. And, I might add, there's no need to give in to what will without doubt be the very great temptation to catch their eye with a look of triumph and vindication as they crack and start playing. Just smile sweetly and sign them up for the next game. You are a *much* more dangerous gamester if you never let people know when you've beaten them, refusing to give in to the pointless vanity of rubbing your victims' noses in the dirt.

The number of people you can work with is pretty flexible. Some of these games need only two players, some need a minimum of five, but the upper limit is simply as many players as you can find while at least maintaining some vague pretence of basic law and order. The games change dramatically in character with different numbers of players, and this itself is one of their most interesting features. When it comes to games, both big and small can be beautiful.

A gender mix is good too—men and women do tend to play these games differently, for reasons that we could argue about forever. A mix of men and women is very different from a single-sex group and, it must be said, games are simply an excellent way for a new group of people to get to know each other a little better. I don't think I can honestly lay claim to any marriages as a result of running these games, but at least one or two interesting relationships have blossomed in the steamy heat of the moment.

Nationality, too, has an interesting effect. I've run these games in five different countries—England, Ireland, Finland, the Netherlands, and the USA. There's no doubt that people with different cultural backgrounds do play very differently, for reasons that I've never really got to the bottom of.

When there are more than seven or eight players, they're best formed into teams. Having teams of players adds a whole layer of complexity to these games, because interesting things start to go on within teams as well as between them. These days I most enjoy playing games with relatively large groups of people formed into teams. But then I typically have a captive audience who are only grateful they're not being subjected to even crueller and more unusual punishments than playing games with me.

Money

As any politician will tell you, you need money to play politics. By far the best thing for getting the job done is *real* money—enough so that it hurts when you lose and enough to buy you a good night out when you win. This concentrates the mind and helps create a perfect mix of excitement, bad temper, and *angst* as each game reaches its climax. You'll need to scale the money pay-offs in the rules of the games to match your own resources, of course, since different people have different views about what makes a good night out. Some of the game pay-offs are denominated in hundreds of thousands and, if you don't scale these down, you may have trouble finding a large enough group of people who are ready, willing, and able to play with you for real money.

A number of the games are played against Nature or the Game Overall Director (GOD), both richly endowed with resources. When the games are played with real money, and unless you are feeling extraordinarily philanthropic and I doubt that you are, you will have to fund GOD or Nature by collecting money from each player. An amount double the walking-around bankroll that each player gets at the start of a game is about right. Neither GOD nor Nature can never run out of resources, of course, so if they hit a little cash-flow problem as a result of the spectacular success of one or more players, a further levy will fall due from all players to finance this.

Some people, of course, don't have any money, while others take the money they do have very seriously and don't like playing games with it. In these cases you'll just have to improvise. Two things are needed to replace the genuine article: fake money and motivation. Fake money is the easy part. You can design your own banknotes and reproduce them on a photocopier. You can embezzle fake money from a board game or steal chocolate money from a Christmas tree. You can buy counters or chips from a shop, collect matchsticks or pennies. As you will surely find out when you first go to prison, more or less anything can be used as money if needs must, although things that are reasonably light and portable are the most convenient. In an interesting game I played recently, designed needless to say by students, happiness was denominated in beer-mats.

This leaves the deep-rooted psychological problem of motivation, solved at a stroke by sheer greed if the games are played for hard currency. Even if real money is not involved, however, most normally adjusted people do enjoy playing games. This means that, provided the person running the games is simply bursting with enthusiasm as I'm sure they will be, the motivation problem tends to sort itself out. Even players without an inbuilt will to win can often get very involved in political games.

If normal human instincts fail to do their job for some reason, or if you find yourself playing with subhuman zombies who are able to chew gum, comb their hair, and sneer at the same time but who can do little else of interest, then you might try a Pavlovian system of forfeits for the losers and rewards for the winners. As far as I know Strip Coalitions has yet to be played, and I am ashamed to admit that I have never suggested it myself. That is no reason at all for you not to have a go, however. The reward that I have found works the best is a bottle of Irish whiskey for the winners, appreciated as much by red-blooded human beings as by zombies, although a good single malt Scotch is a very acceptable substitute. One nice thing about forfeits and rewards such as these is that another sort of game starts as soon as the official game stops and you can claim at least a small bit of credit for this too.

Fake money does, it must be said, have one very major advantage over the real thing—zero notes. In the real world, banknotes worth zero dollars, zero pounds, zero yen, and so on have never really caught on. This is presumably because even an infinite number of them, which would of course be extremely heavy to carry around, is not enough to buy the cheapest thing in the world. In game play, however, zero notes have some interesting and devious uses. Trust me and print some.

Other stuff

Apart from players, money, and motivation, all you really need for most of these games are:

- ordinary packs of playing-cards, doctored as appropriate for some of the games;

- some simple badges for team names (if I am feeling especially boring, I use self-adhesive address labels on which I write names with a felt-tip pen before everyone falls asleep);
- a watch, an egg-timer, or some other chronographic device for timing rounds;
- a blackboard, white board, or a large sheet of paper for keeping the score.

A basic version of many of the games can be played with this equipment. A few others need more stuff—a three-sided soccer pitch and three goals, for example, or a dartboard and darts—but I will cross these bridges when I come to them.

DELUXE DELIGHTS

Going beyond the basics, the scope for embellishing these games into exotic social extravaganzas is limited only by your imagination. And you really must push the boat out a bit when you play a game, rather than just putting on a hair shirt and making do with the basic equipment.

Music

A music soundtrack is simply the most brilliant recent innovation in the running of games, once more the brainchild of student gamesters. These days, a game's just not a game if it doesn't have a soundtrack and, to be honest, even though you *can* manage without one, I now regard a soundtrack as part of any game's basic equipment. There are 69 reasons why, but I'll concentrate on just a few.

The first and most important reason is that soundtracks are fun. Anything that makes a game feel more like fun and less like work is good. At the very least, just play your favourite albums, or those you think most fitting, as background music. Or you can make up a tape of popular ditties that you feel suit the game for one reason or another. Just having background music with games is like moving from mono to stereo sound, like switching from black and white to colour TV, or like the first time you taste really good Mexican food.

But there are also outstanding practical reasons why you should use a soundtrack with games. The first is that music fills the silences in games, just as it fills the silences in parties—and an excellent rule of thumb is that any game should be as much like a party as possible. This gets over those early moments of embarrassment that sometimes set in after the rules have been explained and people set off on their first round of bargaining. Some people just feel awkward getting up in cold blood and starting to do deals with others. Music smooths the slide from the real world into the game and sends out a social signal that something new and exciting is about to happen.

More important than this for political games, music provides a veil of privacy. One unrealistic thing about these games is that all the wheeling and dealing is done in a very confined area, often a single room, where eavesdropping is awfully easy. Once you start to play moderately loud music, little huddles of people can get together in much greater privacy, without everyone in the room knowing their business. The volume control on the soundtrack, in fact, is the privacy control for the game. You can turn the sound up so high that all forms of verbal communication are impossible and people have to pass notes to each other, though this tends to annoy the neighbours. You can have it so high that only a *very* close-knit huddle of people can talk to each other at the same time. The lower you turn the volume, the bigger the group that can engage in simultaneous negotiation. This gives you an important dimension of control over the game without having to intervene personally, lay down the law and boss people around—one knob does it all.

Perhaps the most intriguing use of a soundtrack, however, is to use it to run the game for you. Most of the games have rounds that last a fixed time. Very commonly, as in the real world, these rounds comprise periods when people are just hanging out doing deals with each other, and periods, such as committee meetings or sessions of the legislature, when people make public statements and formal moves. I think of these phases of the game as 'daytime' and 'after-hours'. The formal moves take place in daytime, the wheeling and dealing gets going after hours. A major and unrealistic pain in the butt when running a game is timing these phases of the action and trying to bring people to order at the end of one phase and the beginning of another. It forces the person running the game to keep watching the time, and it can be very hard to restore order after an intense night of bargaining—indeed it absolutely should be very hard to restore order if the game has been going well. If the person running the game has to keep shouting and roaring and bossing people around, they keep being reminded that it's a game and not real life. All in all, timing the rounds of a game manually is very, very boring.

A soundtrack can do the job for you, marking the relentless transition from daytime to after-hours automatically, and liberating both players and GOD from clock-watching and other tedious pursuits. Setting up the soundtrack takes a little work, but believe me it's well worth it. The way to do it is to put together a tape that alternates a really good music track with a period of silence. While the music is playing, it's after hours and people can do whatever they like. Dawn breaks when the music stops, and formal moves can be made. When the music starts again it's after hours, and no formal moves can be made (though GOD can make pay-offs from the previous round during this period). Keep the music good and loud and there can be no doubt at all when it's daytime and when it's after hours. Make the soundtrack as long as you want the game to run, and set the tape rolling at the start of the game—the timing of everything then takes care of itself.

I tend to run games for an hour and a half, so use a ninety-minute tape for the soundtrack. To get in lots of rounds and keep up the pressure on the players, I use two-minute days, while nights last until the music stops—most rock tracks last between three and five minutes. This means making up a ninety-minute tape which alternates a piece of music with a two-minute silence, and I time the two minutes very precisely. I only use music I like—why should I listen to anything else?—a mixture of rap, reggae and country music, with some obscure tracks from the days of my youth thrown in for good measure. Of course players who know the music well will have an advantage because they know how long each night is going to last. This seems to me to be knowledge that is justly rewarded, but you can use a more varied mix of music if you don't want to favour one particular group of music fans. The occasional slow track is OK, I suppose, but we're trying to build to a frantic climax here, so most nights should throb to a relentless beat. Play the music as loud as you can get away with; you want to make the contrast between those drab working days and those steamy,

steamy nights as dramatic as possible. Trust me. Do it. Life will never be the same again.

Lights

As well as marking the transition from day to night with music you can, indeed you should, also do it with lights. Play in a room with the blinds closed. Turn on the lights for a political day. Turn them off for a political night. You might want to leave just a teeny-weeny bit of red (of course) light at night so that people don't start falling over the furniture and hurting themselves as they get ever more excited. Using loud music and a sultry red light for political night, in contrast to bright white light and the deafening sound of silence during a political day, everyone will know, and more importantly will feel, *exactly* where they stand.

Booze

As many readers I'm sure will agree, alcohol makes a big difference too, typically for the better. I've served beer to generations of game players with great success and would just love one of those research grants that would let me oil the works with cases of vintage champagne. One of the best games I ever organized was played by about thirty people in a bar in Holland, booked out for the occasion and, as might be expected, well equipped with a wide range of beverages and a powerful sound system. It is important that the games build to a frenetic climax of panic and excitement and, for one reason or another, the diligent application of alcohol greatly contributes to this process. I have yet to inject too much alcohol into a game. Though logic suggests that there must be a point after which things start to go seriously downhill, only diligent experimentation will reveal it and this point has, to the best of my knowledge, yet to be revealed. It's all still there to play for.

Costumes

Costumes are well worth considering. I could sense the more theatrically minded readers going to sleep when I suggested boring old self-adhesive address labels and felt-tip pens as a way of identifying the different teams, and quite right too. These utilitarian tools do the job but can hardly be said to have any style. While it's not absolutely necessary for players to turn into drag queens before playing politics, members of the same team can give the whole game a bit of a lift if they all wear the same sort of hat, wig, scarf, or *something*. Not only does this make the various teams easier to spot, which is a good functional reason for doing it, but just making the effort makes a big, big difference to everyone's sense of commitment. In a game recently designed by a group of students, I spent the whole time standing at the front of the room wearing a motorcycle helmet with 'Cupid' written on it in large letters and doing absolutely nothing. At least it gave me something to do rather than just standing around looking Stupid. And everyone else seemed to think that this was a worth-while thing for me to do.

Lack of furniture

Returning once more to the maxim that a good game is just like a good party, it should be clear that you must make sure that there's not too much furniture in the room when the game starts to roll. This is not just to do with the damage that might be done to the furniture, though one recent group of student gamesters under my protection appeared surprisingly armed with water-pistols and buckets of water as part of a gun-running game they had just designed. It has much more to do with the sociology of chairs, and people's annoying determination to sit on any chair that happens to be lying around minding its own business. Too many chairs spell death for a good party, encouraging people to sit around looking miserable rather than standing up, moving around and having fun. Too many chairs spell death for a good game, discouraging people from going into huddles in dark corners, from hanging around eavesdropping on the deal-making of others, and generally throwing themselves into the hubbub that unmistakably signals that the game is going well. So take my word for it. Hide those chairs, or cover them with gooey stuff.

THE GAMES

Primitive games

The first two games in the book, Primitive Politics and Free Riding, are about politics without any political institutions at all. They've hardly any rules because they're about making up the rules. They can end in chaos or order; that's their point. We start with a group of isolated individuals. Each must co-operate with others in order to stay alive, but each must beat the others in order to win. These games thus explore the basic need for some form of political system. Many of the most fundamental political arguments concern what is meant by social well-being, who should enjoy its benefits, and which rules of the game are best designed to achieve it. Players will find themselves drawn into these arguments, to which there are of course no definitive answers.

Once we have seen ways in which politics might emerge from the primeval soup, our attention turns to politicians, a species who by all accounts crawled out of this soup very early in the history of the known world. One solution, though by no means the only solution, to the problem of co-ordinating our social existence is to appoint people to do this for us. Notable alternatives to this include anarchy, in which we co-ordinate our lives without any interference from others, and dictatorship or absolute monarchy, in which all power to co-ordinate our lives is given to a single individual.

When we are dealing with large numbers of people, however, one very tempting way out of the 'primitive politics' problem is to appoint someone to organize the co-operation between individuals that is necessary if they are to survive. For want of a better *sobriquet*, I call such a person a 'politician'. Some people are just busybodies who thrive on bossing other people around and will gladly do this for free, or even pay to do it, but we hardly want people like *that* running our lives. Some of the people who make the best politicians may actually have something better to do, and so must be rewarded for their efforts on our behalf. Not to beat about the bush, I call these rewards the spoils of office and they are kept in a central Trough, into which players compete to stick their noses.

Obviously one solitary politician is no use at all in solving the problems we face in a state of nature since we would quickly have a dictator on our hands, charging us the earth for doing next to nothing and caring little as we all starved to death. When there are rich pickings to be had, however, we need not worry too much about the dangers of ending up with only one politician. Many hopeful candidates will want to get their noses into that Trough and will compete greedily with each other to do so.

11

The third game, Candidate, is therefore about competition between politicians for the spoils of office. Each round of the game is a contest between Incumbent and Challenger. The rest of the players are a lower form of life that the politicians refer to as 'Mere Voters'. Each mere voter has a preferred set of policies and supports the politician who looks like delivering policies as close as possible to the ones she prefers. Since mere voters have varying preferences, they compete with each other to choose the leader most likely to deliver the policies they want. Politicians are obviously in competition with each other to capture the spoils of office. Sadly, politicians are also in competition with mere voters because they want to make lots of attractive promises in order to get elected, but then want to forget about these promises, rather than have all the bother of putting them into practice, once the election has been won and the contents of the Trough are being consumed with relish.

Party games

Having seen what politicians do—and it is not a pretty sight I think we can all agree—we move on to look at political 'parties'. These aren't as much fun as they sound, being groups of marauding politicians who band together and daub themselves in similar warpaint in the hope of increasing their chances of seizing power. There are three party games in this book. The first is about competition between parties to win the support of as many mere voters as possible; the second is about co-operation between parties to take control of a government; the third is about the interaction between these two key features of political life.

All of the party games in this book share one rather gloomy assumption about politicians. This is that a politician will say and do absolutely anything, and I hope I don't have to paint a picture of what that might involve, if it helps them to capture the spoils of office. Despite what sometimes appears to be overwhelming evidence to the contrary, however, not all politicians are pathological liars. Actually, politicians do quite often tell the truth, because they know that they must balance the short-term benefits of a profitable lie against long-term damage to their credibility when they're found out. One of the most difficult decisions facing any politician, therefore, is not *whether* or not to tell a lie, which is hardly the issue, but *when* it is possible to tell a lie and come out ahead.

This view of politicians and political parties will no doubt appeal to some. Others may think it applies to every other politician and political party except the one they support. Others again may think of politicians as self-sacrificing altruists who participate in politics only to enact their most deeply held convictions and who would not compromise these convictions by one jot or one tittle in order to bury their noses in the Trough and consume the spoils of office. Altruistic politicians may well exist somewhere on this planet, but the party games in this book are about the rest. Anyone who believes that every single politician on the planet is a self-sacrificing altruist will probably not benefit from reading any further, although the chances of getting a refund on the purchase price are slim indeed and are entirely a matter of private negotiation between the reader and the owner of the store in which the book was bought.

The first party game is about elections, those battlegrounds in which politicians compete with each other for the right to run our affairs. Typically, parties rather than lone politicians fight elections. The weapons they use are promises. We support a party at an election if we like the promises it makes *and* (it is very important not to forget about this) if we believe that these promises will actually be carried out. Parties make promises about all sorts of things and try to find a package of promises that appeals to more voters than the packages of promises being made by their rivals. The problem is that the views of voters are often hard to figure out and, worse, that these can change apparently at random. Parties must change policies to keep up with the changing views of voters but, sadly for them, each time a party changes its policy it also loses credibility and thus some support, as at least a few electors stop believing that the party means what it says.

The second party game is about what happens when the politicians have stopped roaring and the smoke has blown away after a typical election campaign. It's time to form a government. In a very few countries in the world, this is a trivial problem. One party wins a majority of seats in parliament, or one president wins the election, and is in a straightforward position to form a government. In most democracies, however, things are more complex and interesting, since it is typical for no single party to win a majority of seats in the parliament. When this happens a group, or 'coalition', of parties must find some way to agree on what to do if they take office.

A coalition of parties that want to go into government together must agree on how to share out the contents of the Trough. They must also agree on which policies they are actually going to put into practice, given that they each promised different policies to their voters at the previous election and that they all have to face those voters again at the next election. Every party will try to squeeze as much as possible out of prospective partners in the wheeling and dealing involved in making a coalition; but if one party tries to squeeze too hard, it will find that nobody wants to do business with it.

The next game combines the holding of elections and the making of coalitions into a single political puzzle, running the election and coalition games back to back. Parties don't just fight elections to win votes, they fight elections to get into office. This means that a party's policies must not only appeal to voters, but must leave it in a position to do a good deal with its rivals. A change in policy that helps a party at election time may harm it when it comes to forming a coalition, or quite the reverse.

A sophisticated game

Once the party's over and we're into the wee small hours, things start to get really interesting. We move on to what happens when a small group of smart people must decide what to do, but everyone plays their cards close to their chest and tries to second-guess everyone else. Each must figure out what the others are going to do. Worse, each knows the others are trying to figure out what she's going to do. Worse still, she knows the others know she's trying to figure out what they're going to do. And, need I add, they know she knows they know she's trying to figure out what they're going to do. And that, of course, is only the beginning. We're talking about sophisticated games here, games that force the players to figure all of this out without going mad. The psychiatrist and sage, R. D. Laing, put it nicely:

The more Jack tries to appear not to be frightened
> the more frightened he is that
>> he is not frightened
> that he appears to be frightened
> that Jill is not frightened

The more Jill tries to appear not to be frightened
> the more frightened she is that
>> she is not frightened
> that she appears to be frightened
> that Jack is not frightened

The more this is so
> the more Jack frightens Jill
>> by appearing not to be frightened
and the more Jill frightens Jack
> by appearing not to be frightened

Can each become frightened of being
> frightened and of frightening
instead of being frightened
> *not* to be frightened
> *and* not to frighten?

(R. D. Laing, *Knots*, p. 80)

The sophisticated game in this book is about getting your own way in a committee. Committees may seem boring things to write about and they sure as hell are often boring things to sit in but, as anyone who knows anything at all about politics in particular and life in general will tell you, getting your own way in a committee is one of those things you simply have to master on the road to fame and fortune. The committee, which could be running your favourite local crime syndicate, charity, or pressure group, or could be a cabinet running a country or a board of directors running a major multinational company, must take decisions on a range of different issues. There are a number of possible choices on each issue, and the key skill of a successful committee operator is figuring out what can happen when none of these choices is favoured by a majority of members. You know what you want, and must try and work out what the others want, although they're hardly going to tell you this straight out and if they do tell you something you'd be pretty stupid to take it at face value.

Once you've done the best you can to figure out what the other members want, you can set about trying to get what you want out of the committee, using the many (legal or at least undetectable) techniques available to sophisticated committee members. The order of the agenda, various obscure procedural rules, and any amount of wheeling and dealing with other members can all work wonders for your cause. Since your opponents are trying to do precisely the same thing, however, dancing out of that committee room as the winner can involve some pretty fancy footwork.

Coming out (of the parlour)

So far we have been looking at political parlour games—down and dirty games to be sure, but games played in the comfort of a warm dry room. We now come out into the cold and explore political versions of games that many people will be familiar with. Take soccer, for example, a game that is by all accounts quite popular in certain countries. The politics of soccer, or indeed of any similar field sport such as hockey, Rugby, or American football, can be rather sterile. The basic rules are that there are two sides, and that these play a game that one side wins, the other side wins or there is a draw. This is all quite boring to a political scientist, but *what if we play such games with three (or more) teams?* Three-way soccer, for example, can easily be played between three teams on a triangular pitch with three goals. *Now* we're playing politics! *Now* we have incentives for two teams to gang up on the third, for deals to be made and broken, and for all of that other stuff that makes politics more interesting than sport.

While I concentrate in the book on how to make soccer more political, the same principles can be applied to the field sport of your choice, with what will hopefully be wild and woolly effects. What is more, if you move to a circular pitch, there is no reason in the world why you shouldn't play coalition soccer with as many teams as you feel like, and why you shouldn't let each team place its goal wherever it feels like on the circle. The end-product will look a lot less like soccer, of course, but a lot more like politics.

We move from soccer to poker, a different but equally valid form of human interaction. There's a very simple way to make poker political—give each player three cards but force players to put together five-card poker hands. In poker, of course, players like to keep their cards close to their chest. They'd love to do this in coalition poker too but they can't, because the only way they can put together a winning hand is to do deals with other players. Obviously, in the process of wheeling and dealing players are going to have to reveal something about their hands, though a smart player can still reveal different parts of it to different people and find other ways to come out ahead.

From the poker table we move to the dartboard and Killer, a great coalition darts game that is already widely played in English pubs but which, to the best of my knowledge and belief at least, has never been written about before by a practising political scientist. Three or more people can play Killer and, even if they don't much like darts, they'll love the cut and thrust of making and breaking deals between players, as alliances of the weak band together to kill killers then fall apart as they find yet more killers in their midst. There is also the added *frisson* of playing a down and dirty political game against opponents who are throwing what the forces of law and order, at least, are apt to regard as offensive weapons.

READY . . . , STEADY . . .

You've got all the equipment together and really are ready to rock but I'm going to detain you for two more minutes with just a few final words about how to set things up.

Each of the games has its own rules, of course, but in most games it's possible for the players to change the rules if they choose to do so. To stop things getting completely out of hand, however, there is a set of hard-and-fast rules that apply to all games in this book and cannot be changed under any circumstances. (I'll *know* if you change them, I really will, and then you'll be in *deep, deep trouble*.) These rules, the Fundamental Laws of Nature, are set out in the next chapter, and mainly consist of statements that you mustn't steal from GOD, extort money from other players, and so on. You might want to really let things rip by suspending the Fundamental Laws of Nature but, as a matter of fact, pigs *can't* fly and, if you feel like a particularly wild session, you would do better to throw the book away and let it all hang out in any of 1,001 different and interesting ways.

One of the main points about these games is that the players should be left to discover most of the various tricks of the trade for themselves, and believe me every time I play one of these games, players discover tricks that I'd never even dreamed of. The first time each game is played it's actually just as well if players don't have too much of an idea about what is supposed to be going on. If they know too much, they may start playing to a script, and miss out on much of the joy of discovery. The games that follow, therefore, are discussed in three separate ways to emphasize this point.

The first discussion simply sets out the rules of the game and a very general description of what is going on. This should provide enough information to play the game. It's a good idea to start playing straight away without reading any further. The players may not know precisely what they're doing, but finding this out is what playing the game is all about.

After one session on this basis, you may want to consult the 'how to play' discussion for the game in question. This describes some of the main strategies that should have emerged during game play. You will quickly find, however, that every group of game-players is different and that each will stamp its own special character on the games, devising new strategies and tricks, ignoring the tricks that you anticipated, warming to some features of the game and being left cold by others. It's quite impossible to predict all of the variations that might be introduced, especially since an apparently innocuous modification may have very far-reaching consequences. So the 'how to play' discussion for each game will be no more than suggestive. If you find it completely irrelevant for some game, then you can feel proud that you've had an especially lively and creative session.

The final discussion of each game offers a few thoughts on the relationship between the game and the real world. Most of these thoughts are quite speculative, and many will disagree with a lot of what is said. However, while the games themselves are simple and abstract, they are ultimately intended to throw some light on real politics. Of course, each game can only capture a tiny fraction of actual politics. I hope, however, that the processes discussed are interesting and that, by ruthlessly simplifying them into games, they are not trivialized.

By the end of the book, and the discussions of the 'political' ver-sions of soccer, poker, and darts, there will have been enough of these discussions of the relationship between games and the real world for people to get a feel for what is going on. Coalition Soccer, Coalition Poker, and Killer are all coalition games and much of what is said in Chapter 10 about real coalition games applies to these too. For this reason I do not repeat myself by writing about 'Real Coalition Poker' and the like. The main point of these games is to show that you can engage the politics of coalition in very many different environments, pursuing very many different types of objective. Let me make that simple point here, without repeat-ing myself over a full chapter to hammer it home. What is striking, indeed, is how you can turn almost any 'ordinary' game into a coalition game with no more than a little ingenuity. I really do encourage you to have a go at this, keeping a sharp eye out for some of the intriguing political lessons that can be learnt in the process.

In the penultimate paragraph of this introduction I will indulge in a little of the arrant pomposity for which we academics are so well known and loved, although this does involve putting forward an argument that as a matter of fact I do strongly believe in. I have included the debriefing 'real politics' discussions in this book not because I want to, and indeed against my better instincts, but rather because some people appear to feel the need for this type of discussion, and feel in some sense left high and dry if a game just ends and nothing more is said about it. I take the contrary view. If I could explain something properly by writing about it, then that's what I'd do rather than have people play games. To my mind, to try and put the point of a game into words can trivialize it and may well be worse than useless. I regard games as a quite distinct medium, even an art form, that cannot be reduced to anything else. I'd rather read books than literary criticism; I'd rather look at art than read art critics. And I'd rather play games than try to write down what they're about. There are things you learn playing games that you just can't learn any other way, and that you just can't explain in words. These days when I run games, therefore, I just run them and refuse to discuss them. Some people do hate me for this, it must be said, but I've been hated for much worse.

On a more upbeat and constructive note, it is also very important to point out that the descriptions of games that follow are no more than suggestions, possible starting-points for the games that you might eventually play. While the descriptions of the games may from time to time look rather complicated, the games themselves are not. Don't forget that the written instructions for simply walking around on a beach without falling over make this look like an impossible task, despite the fact that most sober adults seem to manage it with only an occasional mishap, many of them without ever having read the written instructions. But please do experiment. Just as some of the most boring meals in the world are cooked by people who can follow a recipe to the letter but have no real idea what good food tastes like, games that follow their written rules to the letter can be dreary affairs indeed. I don't think I've ever played one of these games twice using precisely the same rules, and have been responsible for chaotic disasters as well as screaming successes as a result. Above all else, games do provide a sort of social beach on which we can all learn something, but none of us will learn very much without experimenting. And, since playing is indeed the important thing, let's get down to business.

. . . GO!

2 The Fundamental Laws of Nature

The Fundamental Laws of Nature set out in this chapter apply to all of the games in this book. They cannot be modified under any circumstances. An unlucky player caught breaking any of these laws suffers the penalties described in Law 13. As a matter of fact, the Fundamental Laws of Nature can be applied to any other game, even if it is not in this book. The result will be a political game.

Law 1. Any civil or criminal law, including any directive of the European Union, in force in the country in which the game is being played must be observed unless this comes into conflict with the rules of the game, in which case the rules of the game prevail.

Law 2. All rules of the game in force at any particular time must be obeyed.

Law 3. All dealings with Nature or the Bank must be scrupulously honest. No player may rob or defraud the Bank.

Law 4. No player may (physically) attack or steal money from another player.

Law 5. No rule may be introduced involving a further unconditional distribution of resources from Nature or the Bank to any of the players.

Law 6. No rule may be introduced enforcing a direct payment from one player to another.

Law 7. A player unable to meet financial commitments at any point must withdraw from the game and cannot re-enter it in the same session.

Law 8. Before any game is started, the players must agree on what will signal the end of the game, whether this is a time-limit or some other external signal (such as the ending of a soundtrack or the rising of the sun). Unless otherwise specified in the rules, the winner of each game is the player with the largest amount of money at the moment of this signal, or the only player left in the game if all other players are forced to withdraw. Once the end signal is fixed for a particular game, it cannot be changed for any reason.

Law 9. Any of the rules of the game may be changed by an absolute majority of the players, or by a number of players previously agreed by an absolute majority (see Law 12). The Fundamental Laws of Nature may not be changed.

Law 10. No rule of the game may be introduced that conflicts with the Fundamental Laws of Nature.

Law 11. Unless specifically prohibited by a rule, any form of negotiation and side payment between players is allowed.

Law 12. All games are administered by a Game Overall Director (GOD). GOD's decisions on the interpretation of any of these laws, or on any rule of the game, and GOD's judgements on the behaviour of any individual in the game, or on any other matter whatsoever, however irrelevant and unjust these might seem, are final and definitive. Any new rule introduced will be vigorously enforced by GOD, who will not be concerned in the slightest with what was intended when the new rule was introduced, only with what the new rule actually says. GOD is not liable for any damage caused, whether physical, psychological, or spiritual, as a result of any eventuality whatsoever.

Law 13. Any player deemed by GOD to be breaking one of these laws or one of the rules of the game shall be immediately expelled from the game and cast into the wilderness, forfeiting all moneys held. *Any* further penalty that is agreed by a majority of the players shall also be rigorously enforced.

PRIMITIVE GAMES

3 Primitive Games: the Rules

PRIMITIVE POLITICS

This is a game for 2–2,000,000,000 players of all ages. It should last anywhere from here to eternity (average one hour).

Like all of the very best games Primitive Politics is easy to describe but hard to play. It could well be the nastiest game in this book. Essentially, Primitive Politics is rather like poker without the cards. In each round Nature supplies some of her fruits to the world at large. The players bid to capture these fruits but only one player can enjoy them. In order to exploit Nature effectively, the players must co-operate. In order to win, a player must exploit the co-operation of others.

EQUIPMENT

The equipment needed is lots of money, a table and a Trough, or other similar container. The money should preferably be real, though imaginary money will do at a pinch. The game, however, is quite, quite, different when played for imaginary money. The Trough should ideally be real too, but an imaginary one will do.

BASIC RULES

1. One of the players, or GOD, takes the role of Nature. Nature puts the Trough on the table.

2. At the start of each round, each player pays dues of 20,000 to Nature in order to stay alive. Players unable to pay their dues must leave the game. Nature throws all of these dues in the Trough.

3. Nature, whose riches are unbounded, whose interests transcend those of the players and who consequently cares nothing at

all for money, doubles the money in the Trough, tossing an amount into the Trough equal to the total dues paid by the players.

4. Nature now auctions the contents of the Trough to the players. The minimum bid is 10,000 and any player can bid any amount over this but must place the amount of each bid, in cash, on the table. To raise a previous bid, the additional cash corresponding to the increased bid must be placed on the table.

5. The auction ends when no further bid has been made after Nature has asked three times for one. Nature then gives the entire contents of the Trough to the player making the highest bid and takes all of the bids that are on the table for herself. (This is the rule and, even though Nature does indeed care nothing at all about money, she must abide by the rules like everyone else.)

6. While players may do whatever deals they like with each other, Nature will only accept bids from, and will only give the contents of the Trough to, a single player.

7. The next round begins as specified in rule 2.

VARIATIONS

Once players have got the hang of the basic game, any or all of the following variations can be introduced.

A. *The level playing-field*. Each player is required to start the game with an identical amount of money, say 200,000. Reducing the size of the initial bankroll relative to the dues paid each round produces shorter, riskier, more urgent games.

B. *Le brown bag*. This variation requires a brown paper bag as an additional piece of equipment. Instead of doubling the dues in the Trough as in rule 3, Nature slides any amount of money whatsoever, at her absolute discretion, into a brown paper bag and puts this into the Trough instead. The players bid for the contents of the Trough, including those of the brown bag, inside which they are absolutely forbidden to look, on pain of being turned into stone by Nature.

C. *The sealed bid*. This variation requires brown envelopes for each player as additional pieces of equipment. Instead of the players bidding in public, as in rules 4 and 5, the auction is conducted by sealed bid. Each round, each player must put a brown envelope on the table. This envelope contains the amount that the player is bidding for the Trough, which may be absolutely nothing. Nature sells the Trough to the highest bidder and collects all bids as before.

FREE RIDING

This is a game for 3–300 players of all ages. It should last about an hour and a half.

Free-Riding is about how to pay for public projects that everyone can enjoy whether or not they pay for them. The possibilities for anti-social and even worse behaviour are considerable.

EQUIPMENT

The equipment needed is lots of money, some plain brown envelopes, some paper, and a regular pack of fifty-two playing-cards with no jokers. If imaginary money is used, then each player should be given 100,000 to start with; a liberal number of zero notes should be included. If real money is used, then all figures in the rules may need to be scaled up or down by prior agreement between the players, according to how brave, foolish and/or rich they are.

BASIC RULES

1. One of the players, or GOD, takes on the role of Nature.
2. If there are more than seven players then the players are formed into seven tribes, which need not be of equal size. There is no advantage in having any particular name or in being a member or a larger, or even a smaller, tribe. Nature chooses one player to be Boss and gives each tribe a name from the following list:

- Rastas
- Rappers
- Rockabillies
- Headbangers
- Soul Sisters
- Blues Brothers
- Village People

If the players are for some reason displeased with these tribal names, then there is little that can be done to stop them from choosing an alternative set that sits more easily with how they feel about the world. Serious thought should be given to the choice of names, however; these are not to be taken lightly.

3. Nature shuffles the cards enthusiastically and deals them face down to each of the tribes. Some may end up with more cards than others. However unfair this may seem at first sight, please note not only that fairness has nothing at all to do with politics but also that it doesn't matter very much in the scheme of things if some players have more cards than others.

4. The tribes now peruse their cards, which tell them how they feel about four key areas of public spending, keeping these cards, *very* close to their chests. All number cards count at face value, aces low. Court cards represent the aristocracy and, for reasons that the players will immediately understand, are worth next to nothing— one each to be precise. Each tribe adds up the value of the cards it holds in each suit to find out how it feels about:

- social welfare (hearts)
- defence (clubs)
- public works (spades)
- industrial development (diamonds)

Each tribe feels most strongly about the suit with the highest face value, least strongly about the suit with lowest face value, and prefers the suit with the second highest value to the suit with the third highest value. If two suits have equal face value, then these share equal ranking.

5. The tribes are going to be deciding whether or not various projects that are up for consideration will receive public funding. They get a pay-off of 50,000 if a project in their first-ranked area is funded; they get 30,000 from a project in their second-ranked area, 20,000 from one in their third-ranked area, and nothing at all from a funded project in their fourth-ranked area. If two policy areas have equal ranking, then each gives a pay-off that is an average of this and the next lowest ranking.

Thus, for example, if a tribe holds a hand in which the suits rank in value, clubs, diamonds, spades, hearts, then its pay-offs from funded projects are as in Table 3.1.

Table 3.1

Rank	Suit	Policy area	Budget
1	Clubs	Defence	50,000
2	Diamonds	Industrial development	30,000
3	Spades	Public works	20,000
4	Hearts	Social welfare	zero

Table 3.2

Rank	Suit	Policy area	Budget
1=	Hearts	Social welfare	40,000
1=	Diamonds	Industrial development	40,000
3	Spades	Public works	20,000
4	Clubs	Defence	zero

If a tribe holds a hand in which the suits rank in value, hearts and diamonds equal first, spades, clubs, then its pay-offs from funded projects are as in Table 3.2.

6. Tribal Bosses write their ranking of each type of project on a piece of paper. Only bad things can happen to tribes if others see their cards or rankings. Players then memorize the rankings of their tribe and give both the piece of paper and the playing-cards back to Nature, who checks that they are not lying or deluded about the face value of their cards, incapable of adding up, or otherwise deranged. If at any time in the game a player suffers a bout of amnesia and forgets these values, she can ask Nature privately to refresh her memory.[1]

7. Nature shuffles the cards and places these face down in a pile. She turns over the top ten cards from the pile and places them in a line in front of her. In doing this she is announcing an agenda of ten public projects. Each card represents a project that needs

---

[1] If Nature is impatient to get the action going, as Nature so often is, then an arbitrary set of project rankings can be devised and written on slips of papers before the game starts. There is then no need to deal cards to settle project rankings, which can just be shown briefly by Nature to each tribe so as to allow them to be memorized. In deciding to do this, the advantages of speed must be set against the possibility that the players will feel that Nature is manipulating them for some Machiavellian purpose.

funding. The suit shows what the project is about. Thus a club is a defence project; a heart is a social welfare project, and so on. The first card turned up is the first project on the agenda, the second card turned up is the second project, and so on. If a day and night soundtrack is being used, Nature starts the music as soon as she has dealt the agenda.

8. The tribes now have a five-minute political day (or until the end of the first political day if a soundtrack is being used) to fund the first project. The total cost of each project depends upon the number of tribes in the game as shown in Table 3.3.

Each tribe places its contribution to the project in question in a brown envelope and hands this to Nature. Tribes may place any amount they like into the brown envelope, including absolutely nothing at all. The zero notes, of course, will come in handy for making zero (or indeed any other) bids. Before bidding, tribes may well want to discuss their bids with others.

9. All tribes must hand an envelope to Nature before the end of the political day. Any who fail to do this will be publicly denounced by Nature and receive no pay-offs for the project in question, even if this is funded. Tribes wishing to make no contribution at all, quite an understandable thing to want to do, should hand Nature an envelope either with nothing in it, or with only zero notes in it.

10. At the end of the political day, or when all the tribes have handed in an envelope if this is sooner, Nature opens the envelopes and adds up the total amount contributed. If this equals or exceeds the cost of the project (see rule 8), then the project is funded. If it is less than the cost of the project, then the project is not funded. Either way, Nature phlegmatically keeps all contributions.

Table 3.3

Number of tribes	Cost of each project
7	100,000
6	100,000
5	75,000
4	60,000
3	50,000

11. The next project under consideration is now up for funding, and play continues as at rule 8.

12. If a project is funded, Nature gives each tribe a brown envelope. Inside this is a sum of money equalling the value of the funded project to the tribe concerned, as specified in rule 5.[2] If a project is not funded, then Nature merely empties the envelopes before returning these to the tribes.

13. The game ends according to Law 8 of the Fundamental Laws of Nature.

VARIATION

Voting on funding

Replace rules 8–10 with Variation A. Pay-offs remain as in rule 12.

A. Instead of funding each project by making sealed bids, the Tribal Bosses vote on funding for each project. A project is funded if it receives more votes for it than against it. If funding for a project is not approved before the end of a political day, then it falls and the next project comes under discussion. If funding is approved for a project, then its costs are shared equally by the tribes, each of which pays 25,000.

CANDIDATE

Candidate is a game for 5–500 players of all ages although it can be pretty boring with less than seven. It should last about an hour and a half.

It is a game about people who make a fat living out of satisfying the desires of others. Unlike cold beer, chilli-cheese corn bread, or any other satisfying commodity that can be bought and sold in the

---

[2] Nature may make things run more smoothly by having two sets of brown envelopes, each set being labelled with the name of each tribe. The first set is distributed to the tribes to allow them to make their first bids. Nature uses the period while players are bargaining to fill the second set of envelopes with pay-offs in anticipation of the project being funded—if the project fails the envelopes can easily be emptied again. After this, Nature just has to ensure that the tribes have one set of envelopes, and she another, at any stage of the game. She can while away the long political nights by stuffing envelopes with potential pay-offs, all of which she will know in advance once she knows how the cards have been dealt.

market-place, however, an entire government is needed to produce the things that people want in this game. The game is thus about how rival candidates for office compete with each other to take control of entire governments. They try to convince sane people to let them do this by making promises about all of the good things that they will do if they're allowed to get their hands on those levers of power.

EQUIPMENT

The equipment needed to play Candidate involves lots of money, some plain brown envelopes, some paper, and a pack of playing-cards minus jokers. If imaginary money is used, then each player should be given 200,000 to start with. If real money is used, then all figures in the rules may need to be scaled up or down by prior agreement between the players.

BASIC RULES

1. One of the players, or GOD, takes on the role of Nature.

2. If there are more than seven players then the players are formed into seven crews, which need not be of equal size. In this event, Nature designates one player to be Crew Boss. Nature gives each crew a name from the following list:

- Hipsters
- Flipsters
- Finga Poppin' Daddies
- Rastas
- Rappers
- Rude Boys
- Rockabillies

(Please refer to rule 2 of Free Riding for some thoughts on the al-location of names.)

3. Before the game can start one of the crews is selected to be Incumbent. This is the crew with the oldest and/or the wisest boss of them all. In the event of any dispute over this, the initial Incumbent is chosen by GOD, either by throwing a seven-sided dice or cutting cards.

4. One of the crews is selected to be Challenger. This is the crew with the most ambitious and/or thick-skinned boss. In the event of any disagreement on this matter, although in practice this is very rare, Challenger is chosen by GOD in the same arbitrary and capricious manner as Incumbent. The rest of the players are Mere Voters, who must pretend to be glad that they have chosen to be neither Incumbent nor Challenger at this stage of the game, despite the fact that they will subsequently leap at the chance to be either.

5. Nature shuffles the cards and deals them face down to each of the crews, including those who are Incumbent and Challenger. Some crews may end up with more cards than others. However unfair this may seem at first sight, the crews, if they consult their consciences about the matter, will realize, first, that fairness is something earnestly to be striven for but rarely achieved in politics and, second, that it doesn't matter in the slightest to this game if some players have more cards than others.

6. The crews now look at their cards, which tell them how they prefer to allocate a budget between four key areas of public spending, keeping these cards *very* close to their chests. (Aces are low; court cards represent the aristocracy and, as might be expected, are very valuable indeed, scoring ten points each.) Each crew adds up the value of the cards it holds in each suit to find out how it feels about:

- social welfare (hearts)
- defence (clubs)
- public works (spades)
- industrial development (diamonds)

Each crew feels most strongly about the suit with the highest value, least strongly about the suit with lowest value, and prefers the suit with the second highest value to the suit with the third highest value. If two suits have equal value, then they share equal ranking.

7. The crews are going to be deciding between them how to allocate a public budget of 100,000 between policy areas. Each crew prefers to allocate 50,000 to its first-ranked policy area, to give 30,000 to its second-ranked policy area, 20,000 to its third-ranked policy area, and nothing at all to its fourth-ranked area. If

two policy areas have equal ranking, then the crew prefers to allocate a sum to each that is an average of this and the next lowest ranking.

Thus, for example, if a crew holds a hand in which the suits rank in value, hearts, diamonds, spades, clubs, then its ideal public budget is shown in Table 3.4.

If a crew holds a hand in which the suits rank in value, hearts, spades, and then diamonds and clubs equal third, then its ideal public budget is set out in Table 3.5.

8. Crew Bosses write their ideal budgets on a piece of paper. Only bad things can happen to a crew if other players see its cards or ideal budget. Players then memorize the budgets of their crew and give both the piece of paper and the playing-cards to Nature, who checks that they are neither lying nor deluded about the face value of their cards, and are neither incapable of adding up nor deranged. If at any time in the game a player suffers a bout of amnesia and forgets these values, then she can ask Nature privately to refresh her memory. Nature may, or may not, oblige, at her absolute discretion.

9. GOD now starts the music if a day-and-night soundtrack is being used.

Table 3.4

Rank	Suit	Policy area	Budget
1	Hearts	Social welfare	50,000
2	Diamonds	Industrial development	30,000
3	Spades	Public works	20,000
4	Clubs	Defence	zero

Table 3.5

Rank	Suit	Policy area	Budget
1	Hearts	Social welfare	50,000
2	Spades	Public works	30,000
3=	Diamonds	Industrial development	10,000
3=	Clubs	Defence	10,000

10. A period of Hubbub now takes place. This lasts five minutes, or a political day and night. During this time any player may talk to any other, in public or in private. Mere Voters will probably want to lobby both Incumbent and Challenger, revealing as much or as little about their own private desires as they see fit, in an attempt to influence the promises that each is about to make. The best-dressed member of each crew is designated as the crew's lobbyist. While being lobbied, both Incumbent and Challenger must smile and shake lobbyists' hands a lot, however distasteful they might find this. Both Incumbent and Challenger are of course allowed to say things to lobbyists that they do not really mean.

11. After the Hubbub come the Speeches. Incumbent has two minutes, or a political day, to make a speech announcing a set of policy promises to the voters. The speech may be in a language Mere Voters understand, or not, although it must be in some official human language. The promises may be very vague or very specific; obviously they need bear no relation at all to what Incumbent actually intends to do if successful in winning the impending election. Mere Voters then have three minutes, or a political night, to question Incumbent on these promises. (If a day-and-night soundtrack is being used and the music is thumping out at a decent volume, then Mere Voters will need to cluster around Incumbent to ask questions and not all of them will hear the answers.)

12. Challenger then has a similar two-minute political day to make promises, followed by a similar three-minute political night to answer questions.

13. There is now something that both Incumbent and Challenger refer to as a 'F***ing Election', which involves Mere Voters, Incumbent, and Challenger all voting by secret ballot. Each crew writes the name of its favoured candidate on a piece of paper and puts this in an envelope. In addition, the year's taxes of 50,000 must be paid in the envelope (after all, there is no representation without taxation). Each crew boss gives the envelope to Nature.

14. After two minutes (or at the end of a political day) Nature counts the votes. Any crew failing to vote and/or pay taxes will be publicly denounced by Nature, will be looked at askance by the other payers, will have no vote, and will receive no pay-off whatsoever for the election in question, regardless of the budget decided. The candidate with the most votes is declared the new Incumbent.

15. While Nature is counting the votes, Mere Voters amuse themselves as they see fit while Incumbent and Challenger write down on a piece of paper the budget that they *actually* intend to enact if elected, identifying how they will allocate the 100,000 between the four types of project. As indicated earlier, this budget allocation need bear no relation whatsoever to any statement that has previously been made by any candidate.

16. The Moment of Truth has now arrived. The budget of the new Incumbent is revealed. The budget of the losing candidate must be destroyed and *under no circumstance* can it be revealed. If the loser's envelope is not actually eaten by Nature, it must be shredded, vaporized, or disposed of in some equally secure way. The losing candidate now becomes a Mere Voter and the crew concerned must henceforth comport itself in a manner befitting this lowly status.

17. Nature pays off Mere Voters and Incumbent in brown envelopes, as follows. If the budget allocation for a project is more than a Mere Voter desires, then Nature pays the Mere Voter the sum of money he or she desires. If the budget allocation for a project is as much as, or less than, the Mere Voter desires, then Nature pays the Mere Voter the budget allocation for the project. In other words, for each project, Nature pays each Mere Voter either the sum the Mere Voter desires or the budget allocation, whichever is the less. As is only fair, the new Incumbent gets a little bonus from Nature in her brown envelope for being so clever as to win the election—a Pittance of 30,000 to be precise.

18. A new Challenger is selected according to rule 4 from among the crews who have not yet been Challenger or Incumbent and play resumes under rule 10. Nature may find it less disruptive to calculate and make the pay-offs during the first political night of this next round.

19. If every crew has been either Incumbent or Challenger and if, as is only very rarely the case, the players still have the stomach for more, then every crew gets one more chance.

20. The game ends according to Law 8 of the Fundamental Laws of Nature.

4 Playing Primitive Games

PLAYING PRIMITIVE POLITICS

Conflict and co-operation

It will quickly become clear that some form of co-operation between players is necessary if they are not all to lose money all of the time. Superficially, there might seem to be an obvious point at which bidding should stop—when the highest bid reaches the value of the Trough. But this is a snare and a delusion. Bids on the table are gone forever, since this is not an auction in any normal sense of the word and all bids are forfeit. Once you get involved in bidding, what is left for you to decide is whether raising your bid is potentially profitable.

Imagine five players and a Trough that is therefore worth 200,000. Towards what you think is the end of a hard-fought bidding war, you bid 180,000. Some darn rival bids 190,000. You can't get your 180,000 back, so the real cost of bidding 200,000 for the 200,000 Trough is actually only the 20,000 it takes to raise your bid from 180,000 to 200,000. If you win with this bid, you've done quite well. Before you raise your bid you stand to lose 200,000 on the game—your 20,000 dues and your 180,000 bid. If you bid 200,000 and do win the contents of the Trough, you only lose your 20,000 dues.

The problem, of course, is that your rival won't let you get away that easily. Put yourself in her shoes. If she doesn't bid again, she loses the value of her 190,000 bid, plus her 20,000 dues—210,000 in all. If she makes a winning bid of 210,000, on the other hand, this means losing only 30,000, which she might ruefully regard as a bargain at this stage.

You don't have to be a mathematical genius to see that, fiendishly, there is no 'natural' point in this game at which the bidding should stop. If the bids are in units of 10,000 and if there are two people left in the bidding, for example, then every new bid makes a potential net profit of 180,000 when the prize is a 200,000

Trough, since each bid for the Trough costs each player who is still in the bidding just a 20,000 raise. The same is still true, sad to say, even if bids spiral up to the trillions. Players bidding against each other are locked into a diabolical sequence of bid and counterbid that can only end in disaster.

One alternative, taking all of this into account, is not to bid at all. This is of course an extremely conservative and boring strategy which will, quite rightly, lower you more than somewhat in the esteem of your fellow players. Play it if you like, but the net result is a dreary decline into oblivion at the rate of 20,000 in dues for each game.

Don't do it! Think big! There is plenty of lovely money to be made in this game, since Nature will be matching the dues paid by the players. The group's collective resources are potentially increasing all the time if only they can figure out the best way to exploit Nature.

One obvious way to do this is for all of the players to co-operate. If they all get together and agree that one of them will bid the minimum of 10,000 for the Trough, that nobody else will bid, and that they will divide the profits between them, then they can all make a handsome profit. If there are ten players, for example, then the Trough will be worth 400,000—200,000 from the ten players in dues and a matching 200,000 from Nature. If all ten club together and chip in 1,000 each to bid 10,000 between them, then share the contents of the Trough out at 40,000 each, each will make a handsome net profit of 39,000 every round. Not bad for a few minutes' work at the gaming-table but, not surprisingly, this is not as simple as it might seem at first sight.

First, there is only one ultimate winner according to Law 8 of the Fundamental Laws of Nature. This means that someone, sooner or later, will break ranks and double-cross the others. Second, not only is there a big incentive to double-cross the others, but it is very, very easy to do this. If all players decide they will share the contents of the Trough between them, then every one of them has an incentive to back out of such a deal.

Imagine that ten players have got together into a cartel as I have just suggested and agreed to share the contents of the Trough. They nominate one of their number to make the bid but, as soon as the bid is made, one of the cartel breaks ranks and makes a counterbid of 20,000, reminding the rest of the chaos and disaster that ensues if they launch into a cycle of competitive counterbidding. The renegade might even claim that she will never break ranks again, promising that this was a one-off smash-and-grab raid in the Trough. Since no deals are binding, there is nothing to stop any member of the cartel doing this.

Faced with such a renegade, the others in the group are faced with an interesting set of possibilities. They can cut their losses, letting the renegade take the whole Trough and hoping to renegotiate the deal next time. The renegade will make a huge one-off profit at the expense of the others. If it is generally expected that this will be the response of the cartel, however, then this provides a massive incentive to be a renegade and the cartel seems doomed to fail.

A more promising way forward is for the rest of the cartel to exploit the fact that, collectively, they have far more resources than any individual renegade. Cartel members will also be aware that this superiority may not continue for long if they allow a renegade to reap the rewards of a major smash-and-grab raid on the Trough. Having more resources for the time being, at least, they may therefore decide to destroy the renegade in a bidding war and force her out of the game at the first hint of treason. This will be expensive in the short term, but will allow a profitable deal to be set up in the longer term. Perhaps the most valuable pay-off from adopting this strategy is that potential renegades may in future be deterred by the ruthless scorched-earth policy used by members of the cartel facing their first defection.

Thoughts on threats

Cheaper and less messy than actually blowing away the renegade, of course, is *threatening* to blow her away. The cartel bids, some renegade bids against them, reminding them of the dangers of escalation; the cartel then bids against the renegade, at the same time making one of a number of possible threats.

To keep things simple, they might just announce that they have thrown the renegade out of the cartel for ever since she can obviously no longer be trusted, and threaten to blow her to bits in a bidding war if she ever bids against them again. This would, however, leave them vulnerable to sniping with sporadic counterbids by the renegade, who would of course simply refuse to get drawn into an all-out bidding war, and would do this in the hope of harrying the cartel into cutting their losses letting her back in.

Alternatively, they could throw the renegade out of the cartel for a certain number of rounds, threatening to blow her to bits if she tries to bid against them but promising to let her back into the cartel if she behaves herself in the meantime.

Another possibility is that they could let the renegade back into the cartel if she pays them everything she has cost them in lost profits, with a small extra payment as a fine. This could be coupled with a simultaneous threat to cast her out for ever into the political wilderness if she ever breaks ranks again.

In fact, once you start to think about it, there is a more or less infinite variety of threats that cartel members can try, some more effective than others but all designed to set up incentives for renegades not to bid against the cartel, thereby allowing them to exploit Nature efficiently and make fat profits.

For every threat the cartel can make there is a battery of possible responses by the renegade. The response chosen will depend on how seriously the renegade takes the original threat, on how seriously she expects the cartel to take her response, on how seriously she expects to take their expected response to her response, and on quite a few other things besides. The key to both threats and responses is their credibility.

Of its essence a threat is all talk and no action. The nice thing about threats is that they are cheap to make and can be very profitable, but this cheapness does have a down-side. Since threats are cheap to make, the person being threatened must decide whether they actually mean something. I can, for example, threaten to tear you in half with my bare hands if you don't do everything I want but, sad to say, your response will probably be to look at me, look at my bare hands, then smile pityingly as you go about your business. You will have rightly concluded that this particular threat is no more than a stream of hot air coming out of my mouth.

Threats must not only overcome the *credibility* problem arising from the very cheapness that makes them so attractive, however. Another part of the essence of any threat is that, other things being equal, the threatener would prefer not to have to carry the threat out. Think about it. If a person actually wants to carry out some vile deed, actually gets pleasure out of doing it, then the real issue is why she doesn't do the deed anyway. Imagine, purely for the sake of argument of course, that I'm a superhuman psychopath and that I not only *enjoy* tearing people in half with my bare hands but am well able to do so. The hard thing is now to stop me tearing people in half just for fun, regardless of how well they behave. I can *promise* not to tear them in half if they don't renege on the deal, and they may certainly believe that I will tear them in half if need be once they see the wild rolling of my eyes from one end to the other of their sockets and the flecks of foam dancing in the corners of my mouth. Their problem now is believing that I *won't* tear them in half just for the hell of it, even if they do toe the line. To be useful as the executor of a threat, therefore, I must credibly be presented by my sponsors as a *reasonable* psychopath, a maniac who gets fun out of tearing apart only those people who don't honour their end of a deal. This may be a something of a difficult marketing job.

In the absence of reasonable psychopaths, however, all good threats are costly and herein lies the rub, with apologies to Dr Laing:

Jack wants to do X;
> Jill doesn't want Jack to do it.

Jill tells Jack
> that if Jack does X
>> then Jill will do something *so* bad to Jack
> that Jack will wish he hadn't done X in the first place.

She sounds tough!

But Jill doesn't *want* to do that bad thing to Jack,
> or she'd have done it already
>> just for fun,
>>> for the hell of it,
> whatever about X.

Jack knows this
> and does X.

He says to Jill
> 'OK go ahead and do that bad thing to me Ms Jill.
>> You don't want to do you?
>>> I've done X anyway so now the damage is done.

> And we both know you won't
> cut off your nose to spite your face.'

Jill knows that Jack knows
that she knows
that they both know this.
So none of this ever happened.

Except X.

None of it ever happened because Jill is an intelligent person who can think past the end of her nose to the consequences of her actions. She would never make the threat in the first place. Essentially a one-off threat, made in private, to someone you're never going to see again, will never be carried out. The person you threaten looks you in the eye, does the deed, and insolently challenges you to carry out the threat. However cross you might be, if you are honest with yourself the threat has only costs for you and no benefits now the deed is done. You just shrug your shoulders philosophically and walk away. It was worth a try and the person you threatened might just have been a moron who took the threat seriously. Actually, since everyone knows that this is what will happen, you don't even bother to waste your precious breath by threatening non-morons in the first place. But people, even sensible people with their heads on straight, do make threats. So what's going on?

There are two reasons why Jill might carry out her threat to do a bad thing to Jack. The first arises if she's going to have to deal with Jack over and over again in the future; the second arises if other Jacks are watching her. Future Jacks and other Jacks are the same thing really. They provide an audience in front of which Jill can create the key to any successful threat—and indeed any successful career in politics—a reputation.

If I threaten you in front of a crowd rather than in the privacy of your own home, then things are quite, quite different. Let's say I don't threaten to tear you in half with my bare hands, which everyone in the crowd would know that I'm not actually capable of doing without much more practice, but just threaten to break your arm if you do something I don't like. It might cross your mind to look me in the eye, do that thing anyway, and tell me that you know I'm not a sadist and you don't believe I'll go to the trouble of breaking your arm now the deed is done. But then you catch sight of the crowd out of the corner of your eye, every one of them watching me with great interest to see what I'll do if you defy me. That makes a big difference. If I make the threat and you do the deed, then I am going to break your arm, my friend. This will be nothing personal. I'm going to break it, not because I like breaking arms in general and not because I can undo your dastardly deed by breaking your particular arm, but because the members of that crowd will take me much more seriously at some future date when I threaten to break *their* arms if they do something I don't like. Once I get a reputation for breaking arms when I say that I will, I actually don't have to break any more arms at all, and in a strange way everyone is better off as a result. I can make threats, people will do what I want, and I'll be living in clover. My reputation for carrying out threats is very valuable to me and, for that reason alone, you take my threat seriously and your arm stays unbroken. That crowd saved you a lot of pain, not at all because I wouldn't dare break your arm in front of them, but because I wouldn't dare *not* to break your arm in front of them, having threatened to do so.

But of course this is all a little simplistic, because you too have a reputation to think about. This is why, when playing Primitive Politics, a cartel's response to a renegade bidding against them can be the result of a very complex chain of strategic calculations. The renegade might drop meekly out of the bidding when confronted with the threat from former colleagues to blow her away. But this is pretty weak-kneed and it's hard to see how someone would go into the business of being a renegade in the first place if she was going to surrender at the first whiff of gunpowder. The renegade could counter with a threat and a promise, saying that she'll fight this one out to the bitter end if need be, forcing the others to blow her away at great expense to themselves, but coupling this threat with a promise to rejoin the group and play ball in future rounds.

If members of the cartel believe her, then they may shrug their shoulders and, with some regret, let the renegade get away with it in the expectation of reaping the future benefits of long-term co-operation without incurring the short-term costs of punishing the defector. Even if they believe the promise to rejoin the group, however, they may think that caving in, even once, sends out quite the wrong kind of signal to potential future renegades. This could well lead to the conclusion that, regardless of any promises of future good behaviour, this particular renegade must be blown to bits and put on public display in order to encourage the others. Players can learn a lot about building a reputation from playing Primitive Politics.

Bigger and better deals

Whatever the fate of the first renegade, this formative episode in the life of the game often puts the spotlight on what was probably a rather naïve deal to exploit Nature. Players realize that they must start looking for deals that are somehow renegade-proof and often experiment with various types of 'self-policing' agreement, all of which have a key *conditional* element at their core.

One possibility is a doomsday deal along the following lines: 'We'll agree to co-operate to exploit Nature by making only one bid for the Trough and dividing its contents equally between us. If anyone reneges on this deal, then all deals are off and we'll revert to a bidding war of all against all.' In other words the deal is a deal until anyone breaks ranks, after which it's back to the jungle forever.

If you're a high roller trying to figure out whether to back out of a deal like this, then the credibility of the threat implicit in it is once more the key. Doomsday threats, in particular, have a big credibility problem—most people who threaten to blow up the world if they don't get what they want are told in no uncertain terms to go away and stick their head in a bucket. Building a doomsday machine that carries out threats automatically when triggered is a neat idea in theory, but in practice most social situations, Primitive Politics being no exception, simply don't offer the technology to do this. Failing a doomsday machine, if you make a doomsday threat against me to stop me from doing something that you don't want me to do, then I just look you in the eye and do it anyway, even in front of a crowd. Your reputation ain't worth a damn after the end of the world.

Having briefly considered doomsday deals, the players may then try building into their agreement a threat to retaliate against renegades in particular rather than the world in general. The agreement would then look something like this: 'We'll agree to co-operate so as to exploit Nature, make only one bid for the Trough and then divide its contents equally between us. If anyone reneges on this deal, then we'll cast them out of the group into the wilderness. If the outcast ever bids against the group, we'll always raise their bid, using our superior combined resources to do this.'

If only the game had no end, then this type of deal might just work. But Primitive Politics, like life itself alas, does have an end. In the last round the game has no future. No player has any incentive to build a reputation, to carry out threats, to honour deals, or generally to behave as a vaguely sociable human being in the last round of the game. All hell is likely to break loose in the last round unless all of the players are real pussy-cats. The knowledge that all hell is likely to break loose in the last round feeds back directly into the last round but one. Since nobody is actually going to carry out any threats or promises in the last round, nobody believes what people say in the last round but one. But this then feeds back into the last round but two. The whole darn deal starts to unravel from the end of the game right back to the beginning.

The fact that a game has an end-point that every player can anticipate is profoundly destabilizing for this reason. If the players want to avoid having a known end-point, then they could agree before play starts to use some device that allows the game to have an unknown end-point. For example, they could let GOD set a timer for a secret amount of time, or play a soundtrack with a duration known only to GOD herself. In these circumstances, the type of self-policing deal described above has a better chance of success.

Binding agreements

We have just seen that deals between players can be very unstable. Worse, there is no guarantee that the member of the group who actually makes the bid on their behalf and receives the pay-off will go on to share the winnings with the others. I have played many, many games of Primitive Politics in which one player, trusted for some reason by the others, has smiled sweetly at some crucial point in the proceedings and pocketed all of the cash. It may quickly seem to the players, if informal deals don't work, that they need some way to make *binding* agreements. This requires a change in the rules, which can be achieved by an absolute majority of the members under Law 9 of the Fundamental Laws of Nature. Such a change might state that all agreements that are ratified in some way are binding, with specific penalties for reneging.

The players will quickly find out that introducing a rule such as this is not as easy as it looks at first sight. They will need to think carefully about a method of deciding unambiguously when an agreement has been made, what it involves, the nature of the penalties to be imposed upon renegades, by whom, and often lots of other niggly little things besides—the sorts of things that give lawyers so much profitable work to do in the real world. While introducing binding agreements might seem to be the answer to the players' prayers after a particularly harrowing bout of two-faced behaviour by a renegade colleague, they will soon learn that they just can't cover every angle.

Slavery

One realistic but unpleasant sight that can sometimes be observed as the game unfolds is the exploitation of a weaker group of players by a better-endowed group. This arises because the agreement to co-operate and share the contents of the Trough need not be made between *all* of the players. All that is needed is a group of players with sufficient resources between them to blow away the others in a showdown. Such a dominant group can do a deal to take the entire contents of the Trough for themselves and threaten to outbid and ruin anyone who defies them. The weaker players will just walk away from the game, even ignoring GOD's commands to sit up straight and face their responsibilities if they can see nothing in their futures but a slow decline into oblivion. But the dominant group could avoid this if, having captured the entire contents of the Trough for themselves, they voluntarily out of the goodness of their hearts and as an act of the purest charity, pay the weaker players back their dues plus a tiny profit to keep them in the game at a bare subsistence level.

This would greatly increase the well-being of the dominant group at the expense of the other players, since only the dominant group would share the fruits of Nature's bounty, instead of needlessly dividing this between all of the players.

PLAYING PRIMITIVE POLITICS VARIATIONS

The variations suggested in the rules are but three of very many that can be attempted. Each, however, has a distinctive impact on the game.

The level playing-field

One of the last words that springs to mind when people think about politics, of course, is 'fair'. Politics isn't fair and there is no particular reason to make political games fair either. If people play Primitive Politics with their own resources and some start the game with more resources than others, then those with the more resources are in a far better position. Indeed we have just in effect seen that, if a very small minority of players between them have more resources than all of the others combined, then they can form a dominant group, threaten to destroy all who defy them, capture the entire contents of the Trough for themselves, and then turn the other players into wage slaves by paying them just enough to keep them alive in the game so as to allow the fat cats to expropriate Nature's bounty to their hearts' content.

Of course while the fat cats have the economic power to blow away the wage slaves in a bidding war, the *power to change the rules of the game* does still reside with a majority of players. When economic resources are unequally distributed in the game, therefore, we should find poor majorities attempting to find rule changes that relieve rich minorities of some of their wealth while still complying with the Fundamental Laws of Nature. The fat cats, however, typically find ways to use their wealth to interfere in the decision-making process, perhaps by bribing a few starving voters.

Players might, however, want to see what the game would be like, apart from being unrealistic, when everybody plays politics with equal resources. This can easily be arranged by starting with a level playing-field. The main effect is to equate economic and political power, at least at the start of the game, in the sense that any group with enough economic resources to blow away the opposition also has the votes needed to enact rule changes. This will of course not in itself bring an end to the exploitation of one group of players by another. What it will do is ensure that at least the exploited group is a minority rather than a majority of the players.

Those concerned to end the exploitation of minorities will need to do much more than start with a level playing-field, however, and will have their work cut out convincing a majority to vote for rule changes that have the desired effect.

Le brown bag

Brown bags full of money are of course part of the very fibre of politics and are useful in many situations. This particular brown bag allows Nature to conceal how much bounty she is adding to the players' dues, which bounty may be precisely nothing, quite a lot, or anything in between. The brown bag variation transforms the game, making it as much a game against Nature as a game between the players.

Naïve gamesters might wonder why Nature would ever put any bounty into the brown bag, but a moment's thought will reveal the reason why. While caring nothing at all for money, as we have seen, Nature is amused by chaos and disorder and ultimately gets bored by stability of any sort. If she always added nothing to the players' dues, and if the players can get their act together with an agreement not to bid against each other, then at least they can get their dues back with a tiny bid or even form a stable agreement to enslave some minority of the players with profitable effect. But if Nature starts playing games with the players, sometimes putting lots of bounty into the Trough, sometimes very little, then she can mischievously vary the level of her bounty in an attempt to destabilize deals between players and in this way create what for her is a far more amusing world. In theory, the players should always bid as little as possible for every Trough. In practice, however, if they don't know the value of the Trough when they bid, then deals have a habit of coming unstuck.

The sealed bid

Sealed bids affect the game in two vital ways. The first has to do with making deals stick. The most effective deals to exploit Nature are typically conditional—specifying this and that reward and/or punishment if so and so does such and such. Deals like this can be hard to make stick if nobody has the faintest idea whether or not so and so really has done such and such. If a deal involves punishing people who bid against the cartel, for example, then this can be much harder to enforce when it is not possible to identify who has, indeed, bid against the cartel. In a sealed-bid system, after all, only *successful* renegades are forced to reveal their hands.

A brand new incentive to be a renegade also arises from the sealed-bid system. In the basic game with public bidding, a cartel that forms to exploit Nature can threaten to blow away the opposition and this threat is made credible by the bidding system. The cartel bids; if there is a renegade, the cartel can raise its bid and, if it has more resources than any renegade (which is the only sensible way to do it), then the cartel can ensure that renegade never gets anything.

In a sealed-bid system, each player makes a single bid which may of course be zero, without knowing what the other players have done. A renegade can easily outbid a cartel that thinks it has the situation under control. If the renegade bid is lower than the cartel bid, then the renegade loses money but stays anonymous. If the renegade bid is higher than the cartel, then the renegade scoops the Trough, makes a killing and really puts the cat among the pigeons. A big enough killing, indeed, may give the renegade the resources to face down the whole group at some time in the future.

For these reasons it is very much harder to put together a successful cartel under the sealed-bid variation of Primitive Politics. The opportunities for any potential renegade are far more enticing.

PLAYING FREE RIDING

Free Riding is quite like Primitive Politics, but with more structure. The bottom line is that if the players can somehow get their act together, then Nature will pour money into the game, paying the tribes, taken together, much more for each project than it costs them. Tribes, however, do not get the same pay-off from each project, while each is free to choose how much it is prepared to pay for any project. Once again, alas, the way to win is to exploit the rest of the tribes, letting them pay for projects that you benefit from. The key, of course, is how to do this most effectively.

Two features of the game make exploiting the other players delightfully easy. First, the pay-off to each player is secret, delivered in that proverbial brown envelope. Second, while the average pay-off for each project can easily be calculated, the total value of the pay-offs for a particular project can never be known for sure, since the fall of the cards will determine how many people rank a project first, second, and so on.

Exploiting the other players can be done in one of two basic ways. There's the barefaced-miser approach and then there's the more sneaky perhaps-not-telling-exactly-the-whole-truth approach. The barefaced-miser approach is very simple, if utterly dreary. It simply involves announcing that you will never, ever, help to fund any project whatsoever. In effect you announce, either explicitly or by your sullen inactivity during the bargaining, that you're going to take free rides on any project funded by other people and pay nothing at all towards the costs of these yourself. The other players will be outraged, of course, but they have only a limited range of responses, short of physical violence.

They might give in to you, but they'd be unwise to do so, since you'll be costing them a pile of money from now till kingdom come. They're better off sorting you out as soon as possible. The most direct response is for each to make the same announcement as you, threatening to keep this up until you give in and start playing the game like a human being. The result will be that nothing will get funded, nobody will make any money, and hundreds of thousands in potential profits from Nature will pour down the drain every game. There will be a stand-off, and only if you are a really nasty sort of person will this go on for too long—you'll just be cutting of your nose to spite your face.

If you're *quite* nasty, however, you might hold out for a bit to see if the others will back down first. If you do this, then they might even try to reason with you and put various types of social pressure on you. If you care what people think about you, and if you want people to play games with you in the future, then you might listen to them and relent. But if you're really, really beyond redemption as a member of the human race, then you won't care much about any of this, and can sit out all the hatred and disapproval with a sneer on your face, waiting for the other players to crack and the megabucks to start rolling in. Nobody will ever play games with you again, of course, and you'll be hated and despised by enemies and former friends alike, but you won't care about that either. What an unpleasant piece of work you must be! If you really are like that, then this book isn't written for you; if anyone who answers to this description is still reading then I must bid them good-bye at this stage, wishing them a long and lonely life.

You don't need to be so revolting to make a pile of money Free Riding however. Moving swiftly from the drearily nasty to the engagingly naïve sort of player, it is even possible for people to make money at this game if they're perfectly honest! But there's no need to take such extreme measures. The fact that your pay-offs are private is the key to your greater happiness. While playing the game like an upright citizen and contributing to all of those valuable civic projects, you can still pretend that you rank any given project rather lower than you actually do. In this way you justify a lower contribution than you'd be able to get away with if the other players knew quite how much you were being paid for each collectively funded enterprise.

Misleading people about how you rate the projects will be especially easy early in the game, when nobody will have much information about how you feel about things. As the game progresses, systematic rivals may be able to piece together the information that you have revealed to them during earlier negotiations and look for inconsistencies, so that you can't be completely outrageous in what you tell them—claiming to place every type of project at the bottom of your wish list, for example. But, if you're careful about what you reveal, then you can be quite effective at keeping at least some of your rankings private.

Even if you understate your rankings so much that the other players smell a rat and figure out that somebody is doing the dirty on them, they'll have no way of knowing who this is. And, if you understate your rankings carefully, then there will still be enough profit left in the game for the others to find most projects worth funding.

Of course if they all do unto you just as you have been doing unto them (and why would they not do this?), then the others may all understate the value of some project to them to such an extent that it seems like a dud and doesn't get funded—even though everyone knows in their heart that the project could actually make a profit if they all owned up to its true value. Actually, if any project looks like a dud for this reason, then either one person is fibbing a lot, or a lot of people are fibbing at least a little. If they want to make any money, at least someone will have to own up to perhaps not telling exactly the whole truth about the value of the project. Those who sit tight and swear blind, black, and blue that they're telling the truth will make more money, however, and this can lead to some interesting stand-offs.

The key to remember in all of this is that your net profit from any project that is approved depends upon the difference between what you pay for it and how much you get from it. What really matters is how much less you pay for a project than it is worth to you. Of course the other players have an interest in making you pay as much as possible for each project but, unless you are very seriously lacking in common sense, you will never pay more for any project than it is worth to you. The point of the game is to see *how much less* than the value of each project you can get away with paying.

You can still lose money, of course, by contributing to a project that falls flat on its face because there is insufficient funding from the others. The first way that this can happen results from chaos and confusion, surprisingly common both in games and in real life. The second way is if one or more of the players sets out to damage the others, as opposed to helping themselves, by suckering them into a deal and then reneging on this, leaving the others to pay their contributions while getting nothing in return.

One implication of this possibility is that the players should *never* agree to pay more between them for any project than its total cost. This has the effect that anyone who does not pay what has been agreed will scupper the deal. Since there's no real benefit in doing this other than the vindictive pleasure of watching opponents lose money, and since it might well be possible for the other players to figure out who double-crossed them, this kind of collapse should not be too common. Chaos and disorganization are far more common causes of collapse.

PLAYING THE VOTING VARIATION OF FREE RIDING

Although it has the same general look and feel as the basic game, adding the voting variation creates what is pretty much a whole new game. For a start, nobody can wriggle out of funding a project if this is approved and everyone pays for it at a fixed rate. For another thing, there's no money being pumped by Nature into this game—the players' pay-offs more or less match the cost of each project. So where is the money to be made?

The key is to remember that different players value each project to a different degree. Since the total value of each project to the players more or less equals the total cost to them of funding it, one of two things is likely to happen, depending on how the cards have been dealt.

First, there may be a majority of players who stand to make a profit out of a project. In which case, the minority must stand to lose as much as the majority stands to gain. The majority can vote through the project, in which case the net payers are members of the minority. This sounds simple enough, but what if a member of the losing minority were to bribe a member of the majority *not* to vote for the project? There will always be some member of the losing minority who stands to lose more than some member of the winning majority stands to gain. Given this, there is obviously scope for these two to do business. It will be cheaper for the member of the minority to bribe the member of the majority, and thereby defeat the project, than to lose the vote and have to pay out for a project that she does not value. But since the pay-offs to every player are secret, finding the right bribe is not quite as simple as that. People approached with bribes will have a strong incentive to overstate how much they value the project at issue, and how much they would lose if they vote against it.

Even if the first bribe can be made, this would be by far from the end of the story. There are quite possibly counter-bribes from members of the once-winning majority who stand to do very well if the project is funded. They may get to work on the wavering member of the majority, or even try to bribe a member of the minority who does not stand to lose very much if the project is funded. In fact there is no end to the invigorating potential for bribery in this game, a feature that can on occasion lead to uproar.

The second possibility is that there is only a minority of players who stand to make a profit if a project is funded. As you might imagine, this situation offers an equal potential for skulduggery. If only a minority of players stand to gain from a project, then some of these must stand to gain quite a bit. This in turn means that they have plenty to spare for bribing one or more members of the major-ity who oppose the project. All that has just been said about bribery will, of course, apply in this event.

In both the basic game and the voting variation, however, perhaps the most important feature is that each tribe may well may get a different pay-off if a particular project is funded, while no other tribe can be sure precisely how much that pay-off is. Exploiting this vital piece of private information is the key to coming out ahead.

PLAYING CANDIDATE

Strategies for winning at Candidate vary, of course, depending on whether you are Incumbent, Challenger, or a Mere Voter.

Incumbent and Challenger
Both Incumbent and Challenger are torn between the craving to get elected and the craving to make as much as possible for them-selves after they've done so.

To get elected, a candidate must attract the support of a majority of Mere Voters. She does this by promising budget allocations that are closer to the desires of more Mere Voters than those promised by her rival. And by being believed. It's no good making even the most seductive of promises if nobody believes you.

Yet we should never forget that candidates have their own private desires too. While the winner does get given a Pittance from Nature just for getting elected, this is not enough to attract people of real calibre into a life of public service, most of whom could do much better if they devoted themselves to business, organized crime, the professions, or some similar, and without any doubt at all more lucrative, pursuit. Quite a lot of Incumbent's pay-off there-fore comes, just like everyone else's, according to how close her actual public budget is to her own private desires. If the actual budget perfectly matches her desires, then she gets the maximum 100,000 pay-off, plus the public service Pittance—though of course the brown envelopes mean that nobody knows either her private desires or her precise pay-off. The more her actual budget deviates from her desires, the less she gets. The ability to fix a budget closer to her own desires than would otherwise be the case is the big advantage to the new Incumbent of winning the election.

This immediately confronts any election winner with a tough choice. One popular strategy is to take the money and run. In choosing this route to fame and fortune, the new Incumbent decides to make a one-off killing and forget about winning the next election. If she chooses this way to go, then she might as well set the budget to match her private desires perfectly. Some Mere Voters may be outraged, of course, given that she promised something quite different in the election campaign, but why would she care about this? Once she's given up all hope of winning the next election, Incumbent can rejoin the ranks of Mere Voters, get some quite decent pay-offs for simply sitting around on her arse all day moaning about politicians, and do whatever the hell else she likes.

The other possibility is for Incumbent to establish some level of trust with Mere Voters, perhaps taking just the public service Pittance and a wee bit of profit for now, but aiming to win the next election, and the election after that, and even the one after that. This way she generates a steady stream of income rather than making a single big killing. This is potentially more lucrative but involves a more complicated balancing act—and after all a big killing is always on the cards and can be saved for some stage in the future when Incumbent gets bored with steady money and wants to retire to some tropical paradise. Incumbent must set a budget that makes her as much money as possible, without appearing to renege on too many campaign promises once the election has been won. The brown envelope that delivers her pay-off will be a big help in this but Mere Voters, if their heads are screwed on reasonably tight, will obviously pay a great deal of attention to any discrepancy between what a candidate promises and what she actually does if elected. Of course candidates will know this and must make their promises with great care, a matter to which we will return in a moment.

Whichever strategy the candidate chooses, whether it be 'trust me' or 'take-the-money-and-run', it will be vital to find out as much as possible about the private desires of Mere Voters. In stark contrast to candidates, Mere Voters have some incentive to be honest about their private desires. If their private desires are close to those of the new Incumbent, so much the better. If they are not, then a 'take-the-money-and-run' Incumbent won't care about the desires of Mere Voters anyway while a 'trust me' Incumbent will actually do something to satisfy the private desires of Mere Voters and therefore needs to know what these really are. One reason for Mere Voters to lie about their preferences, however, has to do with the possibility of getting bribes from candidates, another intriguing matter to which we will shortly return. Some devious Mere Voters who are part of a lobby group (see below) may furthermore lie about their preferences in an attempt to drag the budget promoted by the group closer to their own private desires.

Whether Mere Voters lie or tell the truth, however, the policies that they favour will vary quite widely, making it almost impossible to reward everyone at the same time, and making it almost certain that many Mere Voters will be disappointed when the new Incumbent takes office.

Once more there are two basic ways to handle this, assuming Incumbent wants to maintain at least some credibility among Mere Voters at the next election. One is to be up-front about the disagreement among voters, explaining that it's just not possible to satisfy everyone, but that the policies proposed are the best compromise that can be achieved. If Incumbent chooses this way forward, then the fact that she has to declare her policies first in the campaign means that she probably does have to make promises that are as close as possible to the desires of a majority of Mere Voters. This is a lot more easily said than done, however, as she will quickly discover.

The big trouble here is that Challenger gets to make promises second, and can nearly always find a way, if she's smart enough, to make a package of promises that appeal to more voters than those offered by Incumbent. This is a simple fact of political life, but actually hitting the right package of counter-promises in four policy areas is, again, much more easily said than done.

The difficulty with an up-front explicit set of promises arises when the time comes for the winner to set a budget and collect a pay-off in that brown envelope. If the actual budget is set too far from the desires of Incumbent, then even the losing candidate may get a higher pay-off than the winner! One way obvious out of this dilemma is to be vague about your promises. You will need to say enough to give the impression that these policies will be popular with a majority of Mere Voters. You want them to vote for you, but you will ideally not want to say so much that your supporters will detect every tiny little experiment with the truth that you might care to indulge in.

Of course there are ways and ways of being vague. While you might wish you could get away with statements that you will spend 'quite a lot' on defence, nobody is going to take you seriously if this is all you say about your promised budget. Short of stating very precise figures, you can make explicit-sounding promises such as that you will 'definitely increase' spending on defence—you can say this anyway after the first round is over. You can promise to spend 'between ten and fifteen thousand' on defence, pleading the need for some flexibility to allow the complex act of juggling the private desires of so many different Mere Voters. If at all possible, your more explicit promises should be made in private to particular Mere Voters, rather than in public for all to hear. It will then be difficult for Mere Voters as a whole to put together the complete detailed package you are holding out to them. But, faced with sustained and well-directed interrogation, you may well be forced to face the dilemma of either being palpably vague, or of making a very explicit statement that you can easily be seen either to honour, or not, if you win the election.

Being very vague indeed is perfect if you can get away with it, of course, but just how vague you can be will depend crucially upon how your opponent decides to play things. Faced with an explicit and apparently frank opponent making detailed and popular promises, you'll be forced to be rather specific yourself, otherwise sensible voters will begin to suspect your motives. This is another reason why Challenger has the advantage by virtue of making her speech after Incumbent. If Incumbent is too vague, then Challenger can be more explicit. In fact, Challenger can always be more explicit than Incumbent, unless Incumbent is very explicit indeed from the word go.

Finally, we turn to the delicate matter of bribing voters. Even though this might seem on the face of things to be an exciting and attractive option, you'll need to do your sums very carefully before deciding to go ahead. Don't forget that the real extra benefit to you of getting elected is just a Pittance, hardly enough to compensate someone of your calibre for all of the sacrifices that you make when you devote yourself to public life, combined with your ability to set a budget as close as possible to your own private desires. But you do still get some pay-off if you lose the election, and the difference between winning and losing might not always be so very large. You do have your 30,000 Pittance to play with should you win, however, and may wish to promise a modest slice of this action to certain wavering Mere Voters who might be thinking of supporting the opposing candidate—to be paid on condition, of course, that you get elected. You will probably want to keep these payments quiet, otherwise everyone will be clamouring greedily for their share even if, as is so often the case, they don't deserve it. A more serious problem is that Mere Voters may lie to you about their intentions—after all, why wouldn't they? And since you have no way of knowing how somebody voted, you have to confront the unsavoury possibility that unscrupulous Mere Voters will accept bribes on the basis of hollow promises to support both candidates, leaving them with a tasty pay-off whatever happens.

Without wishing to seem too much of a prude, therefore, I have to suggest to you that it is only very rarely worth while to bribe Mere Voters. It is also difficult to do this without being caught, while being caught will clearly inflict some damage on your overall reputation. Indeed the whole issue of bribery is probably better handled by adopting a whiter-than-white image yourself, while at the same time spreading the occasional rumour that your opponent is in fact bribing voters. It is not only quite unnecessary for these rumours to be true but it is also quite hard for your hapless victim to prove them false. If you use this ploy sparingly, it can bring you some potential benefit at very little cost. Properly exploited, your whiter-than-white public image can thus be used ruthlessly to destroy your opponents. But then, as always, they'll be trying to do precisely the same thing to you.

All of the candidate strategies that we have discussed boil down to balancing the short-term attractions of a 'take-the-money-and-run' approach that leaves you no chance of re-election, against the long-term attractions of being apparently honest in the hope of producing repeated, even if less profitable, election victories. You may even actually *be* honest with voters but let's be quite clear that there is not one ounce of altruism in your honesty. You are honest because you expect to make money from your honest reputation, and you do of course reserve the right to make a major dishonest killing as soon as honesty is no longer the best policy.

Mere Voters

Mere Voters have much less to do, of course, than candidates. However, they do have important decisions to take and must engineer the largest pay-offs they can in each round. Important choices for Mere Voters arise at two stages in the game: when they lobby and interrogate candidates; and when they cast their little Mere Votes.

The process of bringing pressure to bear upon candidates, whether individually or in groups of Mere Voters, involves skills of both advocacy and manipulation. Each candidate will probably be approached, and the most favourable deal extracted in exchange for unenforceable promises to vote for either or both of them. Apart from the obvious need to persuade and convince, Mere Voters will probably get involved in making threats and promises. They can, for example, threaten to support an opponent if a more attractive policy package is not promised. They can even threaten to do this if the alternative on offer is less attractive. Obviously, a cartel or lobby group of like-minded Mere Voters will have much more clout than a lone voter when it comes to making threats and promises—indeed a lobby group involving a majority of Mere Voters can be very powerful indeed. Ultimately, however, you will need to play one candidate off against the other since, if you fail to do this, each candidate you threaten can walk away from your threats in the knowledge that you have nowhere else to go.

Since your private desires are secret, neither candidate will be quite sure whether the threat that you make is really credible—they won't know how much you stand to win or lose from carrying the threat out. They will, however, know that you have an incentive to be reasonably truthful with them about your preferences. This is because, should they actually decide to help you, caroo caray, they will need to know which budget allocations you actually do value. Telling fibs about these to a candidate can thus backfire in a rather nasty way if your lies are actually acted upon. Overall, joining a lobby group of Mere Voters, one strong enough to reveal its real private desires and simply insist that candidates bend to its will, is almost certainly going to be far more effective than going it alone and bluffing.

When it comes to Mere Voting, the main decision facing a Mere Voter is to decide whether each of the rival candidates is either a 'take-the-money-and-run' scoundrel or someone who is, for some Machiavellian reason or another, playing at being 'honest', at least for the time being. This does not necessarily imply voting against the scoundrel, of course. After all, the scoundrel may have just the same private desires as you, so that her ideal budget would be your idea of heaven. It's awfully, awfully hard for a Mere Voter to figure out the private desires of a scoundrel, however, so your decision is best made in reverse.

If you decide, after looking her carefully up and down and listening carefully to what she has to say, that a candidate is playing at being 'honest' for this election, then you have good reason to believe that the promises she makes will be (more or less) honoured. Facing two candidates who are playing at being 'honest' you choose the one whose promises are closer to your own. So far so good.

If you face one candidate you decide is playing at being 'honest' and a scoundrel who looks set to take the money and run, then you have a harder choice. If the 'honest' candidate is promising policies quite close to those that you privately desire, then vote for her. But if the honest candidate is offering promises quite different from your own desires, it might make sense to vote for the scoundrel. You disregard the scoundrel's promises, of course, but figure that her real private desires might be closer to your own than those of the faraway honest candidate.

If you face two scoundrels, then you are in some difficulty. All you can do is play a hunch. Alternatively you can stick a pin as deep as you think might be revealing into each candidate and vote for the one whose squawks of indignation are the loudest.

5 Real Primitive Games

I've already been rather unhelpful and discouraging in the introduction to this book about the value of writing down explanations of what these games are about but, in case you missed it, I'll restate my unhelpful, discouraging, and pompous position here. I really do hope that playing these games can teach you something new and interesting about the wheeling and dealing that characterizes real-world politics. My firm feeling, however, is that the most important job for games is to give you an empathy with certain types of political situation, rather than to explain them or to lay them bare in any kind of systematic manner. If I could write down all of the things I hope you get from playing the games, then I would write them down, you would read them, and there would be no point in actually playing the games.

This is not of course to deny that an awful lot has of course been written down, both by political scientists and by ordinary human beings, about the sorts of things that these games are about. Much of what has been written is interesting and helpful, and some of it is brilliant. But even the brilliant pieces of work typically fall short of giving readers a real down and dirty *feel*, as opposed to a cool intellectual appreciation, for what is going on. To put it simply, you've actually got to double-cross your friends and, of course, your enemies, you've actually got to *be double-crossed* by them, before you really know what double-crossing is all about.

Since there is so much that is lost when we write things down, therefore, what follows in this chapter will inevitably be a very pale shadow of everything that I hope these games are capable of showing. That said, I am forced to admit that some people do like to read something about what on earth these games are to do with, so I offer a few thoughts on such matters in what follows, together with some pointers to the work of those who have provided more conventional treatments of such subjects.

Those who share my grandiose view that, while the rules of games are written down in words the playing of a game transcends words, are free, indeed they are positively encouraged, to treat this chapter as something to be flicked though dutifully before racing ahead to the next game.

REAL PRIMITIVE POLITICS

Playing the role of Nature in Primitive Politics looks on the face of things like an excellent and delightfully chaotic way of winning money from both friends and enemies, cleaning up and getting rich before naïve players get the hang of things and you call it a day. Even though the game is indeed developed shamelessly from precisely such a wheeze, there is a lot of politics in Primitive Politics. The game sets out to explore ways in which a group of people can organize their lives and take advantage of the benefits that they can realize from co-operating in joint endeavours, when stabbing each other in the back does appear on the face of things to be a more attractive prospect.

This and other games in the book, as should already be abundantly clear, assume that people aren't saints. This is not to deny, however, that saints often find themselves playing games too:

> 'My friend, I would like to give you all my worldly goods.'
>
> 'No, my dear friend,
> > it is *I* who would like to give *YOU* all *MY* worldly goods.'
>
> 'My dear, dear, friend, I insist.
> > Not only must you take all my worldly goods,
> > > but you must keep all of your own.
> > After all you must have the best of everything.'
>
> 'No, my dear, dear, dear friend, it is I who insist.
> > To accept all your worldly goods,
> > > and for you not to accept all my worldly goods,
> > would cause me great pain.'
>
> 'My dear, dear, dear, *DEAR* friend,
> > I don't know quite how to put this,
> > > but let me be perfectly clear.
> > > > If you don't accept all my worldly goods,
> > > and if you don't accept
> > > > that I won't accept
> > > > > *ANY* of your worldly goods,
> > > > *THEN I'LL HAVE NO ALTERNATIVE BUT TO . . . .'*

Of course entire books could be written on the games that saints play and I understand that several indeed have been. I have no expertise in such matters, however, and concentrate in this book upon games that are played by non-saints.

When a group of non-saints must figure out how to organize some co-operation that helps them all, and this is the situation facing non-saint players in Primitive Politics, this means that each member of the group would like to let the others co-operate while she lies back and rakes in the benefits of their co-operation without contributing anything at all to it. Putting on an especially large and grandiose hat, it is time for me to make the claim that this tension lies at the heart one of the fundamental problems of politics, if not *the* fundamental problem.

The game starts off with no formal institutions and no formal arrangements to encourage people towards any sort of co-operation. The players start off in what many people think of as a 'state of nature', something that has been a logical starting-point for the work of writers such as Thomas Hobbes, John Locke, and many other of the most influential figures in political philosophy. In contrast to the Garden of Eden, the state of nature that we are talking about here is a miserable place, in which everyone is trying to get the better of everyone else with the result that, in Hobbes' memorable phrase, their lives are 'nasty, brutish, and short'. As the game develops, the job facing players is to look for institutions and other social arrangements that make their lives less nasty and brutish than they are in a state of nature.

Rather more precisely, the game presents players with the problem of how to engage in *collective action* to bring about a state of affairs that everyone in a particular group or society can enjoy, whether or not they contribute anything at all towards the cost of producing it. Enabling collective action is an important function of any political system, allowing the production of such things as clean air, the control of diseases, a legal system, and so on.

Thus most would agree that having an environmental bureaucracy with the job of increasing the quality of the air we all like to breathe is in everyone's interest. Most would also be forced to admit, however, if environmental bureaucrats had to hang around on street corners with collecting boxes asking for voluntary contributions towards the costs of their salaries, that they would quickly find themselves on the breadline. In this sort of case the political system may step into the breach by forcing us 'for our own good' to make payments, which may or may not be called taxes, towards the costs of providing things that we do actually want but would prefer not to pay for if we could get away with it. A major part of real-world political debate concerns deciding which particular things should be provided as a result of this type of political action, and how.

In the game, an agreement between the players to co-operate so as to be able to exploit Nature involves significant collective action. This collective action allows everyone to do better than they would if they all were to find themselves in continuous and destructive conflict with each other. Most of the benefits of such collective action, however, can be enjoyed by any player, whether or not he or she is a party to it. Herein lies the problem—the agreement to co-operate can be enjoyed *even more* by non co-operators, since these people can take advantage of the collective action of others, by bidding in a low-cost environment without having to share in the costs of the mutual self-restraint that create this environment in the first place. This is the essence of what political scientists call *the collective-action problem*. Two well-known early discussions of this problem within the social science literature are Mancur Olson's book *The Logic of Collective Action* and Russell Hardin's *Collective Action*.

There is no government in the game. One of the purposes of the game is to let people explore the arguments for and against various different forms of political regime that would encourage co-operation by regulating players and punishing renegades. Another purpose is to explore the possibility that, even without a *formal* political regime of this type, forms of social co-operation may emerge that can solve the collective-action problem facing the players. Indeed people are forced into such co-operation if they are to extract anything at all from Nature. They must try to organize themselves socially without a formal political regime. They are rewarded, therefore, if they are successful *anarchists*. Two excellent places to start reading about how people solve important collective-action problems without the aid of governments can be found in Michael Taylor's book *Community, Anarchy and Liberty* and Elinor Ostrom's *Governing the Commons*. A review of some writings in this area can be found in my own book, *Private Desires, Political Action.*

Anarchist solutions to social problems are not, in the terms that we are now thinking of them, nearly as exotic as they might first sound. All of us, every day, are anarchists in some situation or another. There is, after all, no law that compels people waiting for a bus or for service at an airline check-in desk to stand in an orderly line. A renegade who joins a long queue at the front cannot be disqualified from the game by being imprisoned, deported, or executed, attractive as these alternatives will no doubt seem to those waiting in line behind her.

Individual queuers do have some sanctions at their disposal, however. If there are large or heavily armed people at the back of the queue, the sinner might be persuaded to step into line by the threat of physical violence. Even when there are no physical vigilantes in the queue, the world is well-stocked with verbal vigilantes armed with razor-sharp tongues. Such people are frequently to be found lurking in queues on the look-out for victims on which to use these, appearing for all the world like ordinary human beings. Verbal vigilantes, of course, will take on with great relish the job of making any queue-jumper's life a complete misery. Being subjected to an interminable sermon on the violated rights of all those poor people who have been queuing diligently since daybreak is often far harder to endure than downright physical violence, at least in those situations in which it is not possible to turn on your heel, sneer, and walk away. Whatever happens, however, the renegade will almost certainly live to jump queues again, despite having broken a tacit but deeply ingrained social agreement about how to wait for buses, for service at airline check-in desks, and for many other things besides.

The bus or airline check-in queue is a good example of the type of conditional agreement that I discussed when talking about how to win at Primitive Politics. Not only is it completely unenforceable by anything short of a level of physical coercion that is generally ruled out by the rules of the game—clubbing the queue-jumper, tying her up and flinging her to the back of the queue for example—but the agreement tends to collapse very quickly when confronted with renegades in any significant number. When a hitherto orderly queue is contemplating a rapidly filling bus that has only a few places left on it, and if at that precise moment a swarm of queue-jumping renegades push forward to grab those places, then things can degenerate into the purest chaos. All bets are off as the most pleasant and ineffectual-looking people perform startling feats of strength, agility, and rudeness in their determination to get on that bus. The boarding gate of a late-night overbooked airliner is another venue where you may be fortunate enough to observe similar exhibitions of remarkable social savagery.

The bottom line in queues, of course, is that there are a number of people who want something and a number, possibly but not certainly smaller, of portions of the thing that they want. Queues allocate the portions according to an unwritten 'first-come-first-served' agreement. Indeed, for those of us who are interested in anarchistic solutions to social problems, a queue is a very beautiful thing to behold. This is not at all because we approve in any moral sense of the first-come-first-served principle, which many right thinking people feel rewards those with nothing better to do than stand in line and why on earth should it be these sorry individuals who are rewarded with the better things in life like seats on buses? No, we marvel at queues because they are a such an elegant physical manifestation of a tacit anarchistic conditional agreement.

Examples of the type of conditional social anarchy exemplified by queues are legion. A beautiful piece of landscape, for example, is a joy to behold if unsullied by the junked cars, rusty old washing-machines, damp mattresses, and those other pieces of personal detritus that can for one reason or another not be very easy to get rid of once they have served their purpose, while not being the type of thing you'd want to hang on to for the rest of your life. As long as a landscape is clean, most people tend to want to keep it clean. This is because tossing the first junked car into a beautiful landscape seems to be an act of particular barbarianism, making the landscape so much worse, for the person who tosses it there as well as for everyone else, that even the tosser is made worse off.

Even this conditional agreement can be broken by two types of social misfit, however. The first is an old-fashioned non-saint whose visual senses have suffered a particularly unfortunate form of mutation, with the result that she either thinks that a beautiful landscape is actually enhanced by the presence of junked cars, or doesn't care whether it is or not. The second is a sadist. As far as collective action is concerned, a sadist is a person who has suffered some form of brain mutation that has the result that she is no longer a mere non-saint like the rest of us, but an actual anti-saint, a person whose sole source of pleasure is the misery of others. Such a person, of course, junks her cars in the middle of beautiful landscapes precisely *because* this causes aesthetic pain to others.

After the depredations of one or more of these mutants, sad to say, the landscape is much degraded, and many may now form the opinion that it is not made *that* much worse by the addition or just one more damp mattress. Tellingly, the smallish additional degradation of the landscape may now seem a small enough price to pay in exchange for the private benefits of getting rid of that mattress. The detritus piles up with a vengeance and the once-beautiful landscape becomes painful to look at for anyone with an aesthetic bone in her body. Everyone, apart from those sadists who are of course delighted with themselves at the ugliness they have caused, is worse off at the end of it all.

Many other facets of social and political life are governed by unenforceable collective agreements, explicit or tacit. Two obvious areas where these are particularly important are the criminal activity (criminals cannot use the powers of government to regulate their activities and enforce their contracts, yet they typically manage a reasonably orderly organization of criminal life) and international politics (where at least in theory no world government can actually force a sovereign national government to do something it doesn't want to do). In each case, social order is maintained, and collective benefits produced, by the same mix of agreement, threat, and promise that characterizes the game of Primitive Politics.

The other thing that playing Primitive Politics can be used to explore is the importance of some type of mechanism for making sure that agreements between players are binding. Such a mechanism is one of the most fundamental of all public goods, advocated even by most of those who want only a very minimal level of government intervention. A system of binding agreements greatly increases the chance that other public goods will be produced. This is because it creates an environment in which deals between players, for example deals to engage in collective projects, are more likely, since it gives some assurance that deals once struck will be carried out.

In real politics it is of course ultimately the government, through the legal system, that enforces most agreements. The interesting thing is that, in those areas of our lives unsuited to government intervention, there is nearly always some alternative system available to allow us to make binding agreements with each other and hence increase our ability to engage in collective endeavours. Returning once more to the underworld, the power of organized crime syndicates is based upon the fact that it is unwise to double-cross the Boss. Agreements made with a crime syndicate do have a way of getting enforced. In its own terms the syndicate is quite right even to take a huge loss if this ensures that some particular agreement it makes is enforced. The main reason for this is that potential future double-crossers now know what to expect and behave themselves accordingly. A concrete overcoat may be an expensive garment to make for a small-time chiseller, but it's cheap at ten times the price if it keeps everyone else in line.

The bottom line in all of this is that Primitive Politics provides the purest illustration of a theme that recurs throughout this book. This is that much of politics has to do with reconciling the mixed motives of conflict and co-operation that characterize our social life. Many of the things that people desire can be produced only by collective endeavours. This provides an incentive towards co-operation. Yet the best thing of all to do is to take free rides on the co-operation of others, letting them do the work while you enjoy the benefits. This puts us all in conflict with each other. While many non-saints are of course primarily concerned to further their own personal well-being, they are none the less aware that satisfying their private desires can often be better achieved by suppressing short-term incentives to exploit others in favour of the longer-term benefits of co-operating with them. One function of political institutions is to structure the behaviour produced by this contradictory set of motivations. Yet, even when formal institutions do not or cannot operate, more informal types of political interaction can develop to fulfil the same essential purpose.

Real Free Riding
Free Riding is like Primitive Politics in many important ways. Both

are about the need for people to co-operate if they are to satisfy their private desires. Both are about the incentives for people to exploit the co-operation of others when they often have the ability to do this. Both explore the role of anarchistic co-operation as a way of solving the dilemmas that result from the interaction of these mixed motives. Almost everything that I had to say about real Primitive Politics could be said about real Free Riding and there is no reason to repeat it here. The books that I referred to when talking about Primitive Politics are also the best places to start for those who are interested in reading more about Free Riding. I can thus be much more brief and confine myself to some differences between the two games.

Aside from lots of details, the big difference between the games has to do with what people know about each other. In Primitive Politics, things were very simple on this score—everyone was trying to make as much money as possible, and everyone was assumed to regard money as a good thing. In this sense each player knew pretty much exactly what was driving the behaviour of the others—making more money. In Free Riding, different players want different things, arbitrarily determined by the luck of the draw. And each player can only be certain about what she herself wants. Any information given by other players about their own private desires is suspect, since players have so many incentives to lie about these desires to others.

This is very much a feature of many of the political interactions we have in our everyday life. I want to sell my car, for example, and you want to buy it. I'm prepared to sell it for 1,000, let's say, you're prepared to pay up to 2,000 for it. We can clearly do a deal, but at what price? You want to get the car as cheaply as possible, while I want to sell it for as much as I can. So you begin by offering me 500. I laugh ruefully and walk away. And I'm serious now, I just won't sell it for 500; I'd rather keep it. Just before walking out of the door, however, I turn around and offer the car to you for 2,500. This time it's your turn to laugh, ruefully even, and this time you mean it too; you just won't pay 2,500.

Where do we go from here? We each know the other has a huge incentive to lie about the bottom-line price he or she is prepared to offer or accept. What happens next, therefore, depends an awful lot upon what I know or assume about your private desires; upon what you know or assume about mine; about what I assume you assume about mine; and so on.

Imagine for example that I've detected a subtle quickening of your pulse when you look at my beautiful machine, a little glint in your eye. I might form the opinion that you really would pay 2,500 for the car and are just lying when you say you won't. You laugh and walk away but I figure that you would of course laugh and walk away the first time that this, or indeed any other, figure is mentioned and are just hiding the real value of my beautiful car to you. I stick to my guns.

In the same way, you may smell the faint but unmistakable scent of desperation about me when you turn down my offer, glimpse that look of panic flickering behind my eyes and form the opinion that I really need the money and would take very much less than the 2,500 I first asked for. You're going to hang on and wait for me to crack, giving me no sense at all of what you're prepared to pay.

In either case we might be wrong, however. The deal may founder on these misperceptions even if we really do want to trade that car.

Or, and this is probably the more common scenario, we may *both* know that the other wants to do business in the general ballpark signalled by the opening offer and counter-offer. Indeed we may know much more than this if we live in a social world in which splitting the difference between these two opening positions is an important norm about how to do business in situations such as this. If we both know about this norm, and both know that the other knows about it, then your opening offer, and especially my counter-offer, signal some very important information. In responding with an offer of 2,500 to your opening suggestion of 500, I may well really be suggesting a split-the-difference final possibility of 1,500. We both know this, are both prepared to accept this, and may wend our way warily towards it in subsequent negotiations. (This is of course one of the reasons why it is so difficult to do business in alien cultures; indeed it is almost the definition of an alien culture that people on different sides of some social transaction don't have common knowledge about such norms.)

Why don't we save ourselves a lot of time, jump straight to that 1,500 and get the bargaining over and done with? We don't do this precisely *because* I know that you know that the initial counter offer of 2,500 signals an eventual agreed price of 1,500 given these norms. And I know you know I know this. Why wouldn't you use your offers to signal a lower final price than you are really prepared to pay? (As of course you did in this case!) We do, after all, want to do business and can't waste our time on this transaction for ever, so we must move things along. But we don't mind taking a little bit of time in the negotiations to watch for that flicker of panic, to sniff for that sweet smell of fear, to look intently for those inadvertent signals that our opponent is running a major bluff against us. All the time, of course, we are trying as hard as we can to control very carefully any signals that we might give off about our own private desires. The key to it all is that neither knows quite what the other will really settle for. The fact that our desires are private lies at the very heart of the game we thus play.

In this way the second game is a little bit more realistic than the first, since real people do desire different things, and I can never be quite sure what it is that you want. Private desires for public policy, just as much as private desires for consumer trinkets, do ultimately remain private. What people tell you about these desires, *even if this is the truth*, is never more than what they want you to know.

Real candidates

Primitive Politics and Free Riding were played directly against Nature. In Candidate, however, there are intermediaries, the candidates for election to a government. The successful candidate gets a small private prize for getting into government in the first place, then sets a big public budget that fixes how the players' resources will be allocated between projects. In contrast to the previous games, it's now certain that some public goods will be produced; this is no longer the issue. The question now concerns how much will be provided for in the budget for each project, and how close this budget will be to the private desires of the winning candidate. While there are many books to read about candidates and elections, none of these, to my knowledge, really puts forward a view of these things that is particularly close to the spirit of this game. A good place to start, however, is Alan Ware's very clear general introduction, *Political Parties and Party Systems*.

Candidates who get elected thus have two sources of reward. One is the prize they get just for being able to stalk the corridors of power and feel like a big shot. We should never, ever, forget what a heady elixir this is, capable of transforming the most run-of-the-mill human beings into something quite bizarre and extraordinary. The other prize is being in a position to bend the shape of public policy in accordance with their own views.

This structure of pay-offs, and the fact that elections are held at regular intervals, means that election winners face an awkward trade-off. On the one hand they want to be elected over and over again. This way they stalk the corridors of power for ever and ever, gorging on that heady elixir and feeling quite definitely the biggest shots in town. On the other hand they want public policy to match their own private desires, even if these desires are manifestly unpopular.

The essential dilemma for real candidates is thus a choice between telling the truth and lying or, to put it more delicately, between telling the truth and not telling the truth. Truthful candidates will figure out what voters want, will promise them this, and will then honour these promises if elected. They will tend to be popular with the voters, and this will help their chances of re-election. Untruthful candidates will say what it takes to get elected, but will be less concerned with honouring their promises once they have been elected, being more inclined to make a killing by doing precisely what they feel like in the short term, at the expense of their long-term elections prospects.

In order to get elected, however, any candidate, truthful or less so, must figure out voters' preferences and try to win elections by promising to vindicate these as best they can. They face three problems in doing this.

First, voters have an annoying habit of disagreeing among themselves about which policies should be enacted. This means that no candidate can satisfy everyone. Indeed, no candidate can even come close to giving any large group of voters everything they want, because there is just no agreement on this. Given this disagreement, any candidate has a major job on her hands, simply trying to figure out a package of promises that will appeal to a decent number of voters.

Second, they must come up with a package of promises that will not be a total disaster for them if they are elected. It's no good winning the election on the basis of a package of promises that the candidate actually detests—it could actually be better to lose the election in this case. So the candidate must identify a group of voters whose private desires are quite close to her own, and then try to craft an election-winning package out of this.

Third, there is the problem of the rival candidate, who is trying to do exactly the same thing. Voters don't just pick a package they approve of—they choose between rival packages, picking the one of these that they like most. So a candidate may come up with what looks like an election-winning package quite close to her own private desires, only to find that a rival has had the same idea, offering something very similar but just a little bit more attractive. It is a sad fact of life for candidates that, as soon as they make a package of promises dealing with a range of different policy areas, *any* package of promises that they make can be beaten by a rival.

The complicated balancing of all these factors is the job of any successful candidate. It is only after the election result has been declared, of course, that the true colours of any candidate are revealed. The winner will then honour promises made, or not as the case may be, and will of course have thought about this when settling upon the content of the promises in the first place. Herein lies the magic of vagueness when it comes to political promises. If you promise to increase spending on social welfare by twenty million, for example, then the public record will relentlessly reveal whether or not you actually have done this. You either do this, or you don't, and if you don't then everyone will know that you haven't done it.

Of course, the game is rather unrealistic in this regard on two counts. Real public accounts can be massaged, and information on other aspects of real public policy can be manipulated, to put incumbents in the best light. Also, in real politics, there is a whole welter of semi-plausible excuses for not honouring campaign promises: 'when we took office the budget figures were much worse than we could possibly have imagined', 'we tried to do it but were thwarted by the man in the moon' and so on, and so on. The game offers no such fig-leaves, makes it crystal clear when promises have not been honoured, and thereby makes politicians *far* more accountable than they are in real life. But the basic dilemma that it poses between honouring promises and, well, not honouring them, is pretty much the same.

The main job for real voters, of course, is to come to grips with all of this and figure out the best candidate to support. As individuals they will be pretty much powerless. But if they organize themselves into pressure groups, then they can have a much bigger impact on the behaviour of candidates who do after all want to get elected when all is said and done.

As election follows election, real voters may therefore find themselves in more or less stable groups, containing people with similar private desires. Candidates will come to know the preferences of these groups, and to cater for these in their promises. Each election will be different from those that precede it, however, both because there will be a different challenger, with different private desires, and because both the incumbent and the challenger will continually be jockeying for position, fine-tuning their promises to seduce dithering members of some group or another from the arms of a rival candidate. Even mere voters, therefore, weak and all as they are, can sometimes be made to feel important.

PARTY GAMES

6 Party Games: the Rules

ELECTIONS

A game for 2–200 players. It should take about one and a half hours. If more than seven players are involved, they should be split into seven crews.

Each player/crew controls a political party fighting to win an election by making promises that fool as many voters as possible. Voters themselves are not represented in the game and are treated by the parties as unthinking zombie-like machines driven by a range of different preferences about which policies they prefer to see implemented on matters of national importance. Zombie-voters will always vote for the political party that promises policies as close as possible to those they most prefer. The possibility that these promises, once made, will not be honoured by politicians does not, for some inexplicable reason, occur to them. Parties therefore compete with each other to find the policy that appeals to more zombie-voters than any other, although the slings and arrows of electoral fortune can upset even the most cunning of calculations.

EQUIPMENT

The equipment required is a pack of cards and a timer or sound system, plus a bundle of money and a badge for each player. Players will also need a copy of the game board shown in Fig. 6.1, plus twenty-one black counters (any other colour, I suppose, would do) and a playing piece for each party. Players may use as playing pieces any objects that they find amusing, provided that these are also small enough to be moved without too much fuss around the playing-board. GOD will also need a trusty ruler.

THE RULES

1. *Setting up the board.* The playing-board shows possible policies that can be promised by political parties on the most important issue of the day, which is taken for the sake of argument to be the level of personal income tax that will be set in the next budget. Possible policies on this matter can be seen in the top and bottom rows of the board and range from 60 per cent taxation on the far left to 22 per cent taxation on the far right.

Above each policy position is a column which shows how many zombie-voters rate the policy position in question as their favourite. At the beginning of the game, and before the political parties have got to work, the distribution of opinion among voters is shown by the shaded squares on the election board. A black counter is thus placed on each shaded square. (These show, for example, that 400,000 voters would most like income tax to be set at 60 per cent, while 900,000 voters would like it to be set at 30 per cent.)

The black counters will be moved up and down to show how opinion among voters changes during election campaigns, but more of that later.

2. Players or crews represent political parties and GOD gives each crew a name from the following list and 200,000 in campaign funds.

- Hippies
- Yippies
- Yuppies
- Beatniks
- Rappers
- Rockers
- Rudies

The election campaign

3. Before the game starts, a time-limit is agreed by the players and the timer is set. Above one and a half hours is a good amount of time to play. More entertainingly, the time-limit can be the length of two albums played on the sound system. The game ends abruptly at the end of the time-limit.

4. The first round of the game is a little different from the others, because the parties must declare their initial policy positions. They do this in sequence by placing their markers on the bottom row of the board on the policy position of their choice. No party can occupy a square which is already occupied by another party.

The order of moves is decided by the length of each party leader's hair. The party leader with the longest hair moves first, followed by the party leader with the next longest hair. The party leader with the shortest hair moves last. If more than one party leader is completely bald, then they cut cards to decide who moves first, low card winning. In the event of a dispute about hair length, GOD will settle the matter one way or another with her trusty ruler.

5. The remaining part of this election campaign, and the whole of each subsequent election campaign, consists of parties jostling each other for position over a period of three political weeks. Each party tries to find the policy which it thinks will be most popular with the electorate. Election campaigns have many surprises but, the closer we get to the great day, the clearer things become.

Opinion polls

6. An opinion poll is held before each week of jostling. *Quite* unlike what happens in real life, opinion polls results are pretty much random. The cards are shuffled and one card is dealt from the bottom of the deck. A red card shows that the swing is going to the left, a black card shows that the swing is going to the right. The election is held after three weeks of jostling; the swing in votes when the election is held will be in the direction shown by the majority of opinion poll cards. In other words, if there are two or three red cards, then the swing will be to the left; if there are two or three black cards, then the swing will be to the right.

Changing party positions

7. After an opinion poll card has been dealt at the start of each political week, in the light of the positions of the other parties and the most likely direction in which votes appear to be shifting, each party may choose to modify its policy position in an attempt to capture as many votes as possible when the election is finally held. In each week of the campaign, party leaders take turns to move

their marker, or to choose not to move it. As before, the hair length of the party leaders decides the order of moves. It costs money to make a change of policy, since the zombie-voters must be told about this and convinced that the change in policy position that has been announced actually means something. If a party moves to an adjacent policy position in any week, then this is hardly noticed by anyone and costs nothing. If a party moves more than one space in any week, then each additional space moved costs the party 20,000 in campaign funds, which must be paid, in cash and in advance, to an advertising agency run by GOD, who has never been known to take cheques, IOUs, or anything other than hard currency. Parties may move as many spaces as they can afford, provided that the space on which they land is not already occupied by another party.

After each party has moved, or has decided not to move, the political week is over and another opinion poll is held, as in rule 6. After this poll, another week of jostling takes place. A third week of jostling, preceded by an opinion poll, follows the second.

The election

8. The election takes place after three weeks of jostling. Each party must pay 20,000 from campaign funds to GOD's advertising agency to meet its election expenses. Parties unable to pay their election expenses cannot receive *any* votes in the election. They remain in the game but are treated when votes are shared out as if they did not exist. A party that fails to meet election expenses in two consecutive elections is summarily thrown out of the game, during which process the other players make speeches saying the nicest things that they can think of about the failed political party.

9. The direction in which votes will swing in the election has already been revealed by the opinion polls (see rule 6). The opinion poll cards are now returned to the pack, which is reshuffled in a desultory way by GOD.

10. The first election results to be declared are those for the side of the board that will gain from the swing in votes. If the swing is to the left, then the first result declared is for the policy position which is furthest to the left (60 per cent income tax). If the swing is to the right, then the policy position furthest to the right (22 per

cent income tax) is declared first. The results for the remaining policy positions are declared in sequence, moving towards the centre of the board.

11. The result for each policy position is declared by dealing a card face up from bottom of the election pack. Court cards represent the aristocracy and, as might be expected, make no difference either way to anything at all and especially to elections; thus no votes are added or subtracted if a court card is dealt for some policy position. Other cards represent the Salt of the Earth, honest zombie-voters who do make a very significant difference to election results. When one of these cards is dealt for a policy position, if it is:

- Ace, 2, 3 then add 100,000 votes
- 4, 5, 6, 7 then add 200,000 votes
- 8, 9, 10 then add 300,000 votes
- Joker then add 500,000 votes

Whatever the cards say, no policy position can be supported by more than two million, or less than 100,000, voters.

People who have trouble doing sums should not find any of this too taxing. This is because the board itself functions as a kind of stone-age calculator. The counter above the position in question is moved after the election result for that position has been declared, to indicate the number of voters now supporting that position. To add 100,000 zombie-votes, hold your tongue tightly between your teeth and move the relevant counter up one space. To add 300,000 votes, move the counter up three spaces in the same fashion, and so on. Thus all people capable of simultaneously holding their tongues tightly between their teeth and moving a counter on a board should be able to conduct an election. Players incapable of doing this may retain the services of a 5-year-old child to assist them.

12. The results for the losing side of the board are now declared. The ten election cards dealt for the winning side are first collected. These cards, *and these cards only*, are then reshuffled by GOD. Election results are declared in exactly the same way as for the winning side of the board, except that votes are subtracted, rather than added, at the levels indicated in rule 11. Thus it should be immediately clear that the counters on this side of the board are

moved down rather than up the appropriate number of spaces when each result is declared.

13. The level of support for each party can now be worked out. Each party receives all of the votes that are in columns closer to its own policy position than to the position of any other party. If there is an odd-number of unoccupied policy positions between two parties, then the votes from those supporting the middle position are shared equally by the two parties concerned. (For examples, see Fig. 6.2.)

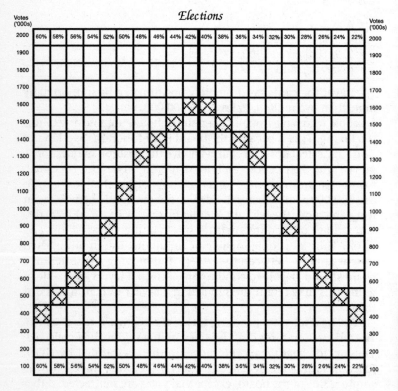

Fig. 6.1   The election board

The pay-off

14. Once the vote totals for each party have been declared, parties receive a contribution from GOD towards their campaign expenses for the next election. This contribution is in direct proportion to the number of votes the party won at the election that has just been held, at the rate of 10,000 for every million votes.

15. Another election campaign starts immediately. The starting-positions of the parties at the beginning of the next election campaign are those that they occupy at the time of the election that has just been held. Play therefore recommences at rule 6. Parties now move in the order of the votes totals that they won in the previous election, with the party winning the most votes moving first. If two or more parties win the same number of votes, then the party leader with the most overweening ambition moves first.

16. When the time-limit is up, a snap election is held. No cards are dealt, and votes for each policy position are those shown on the

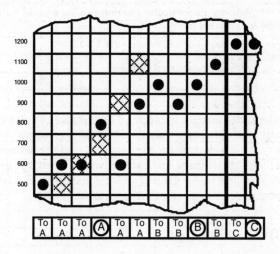

Fig. 6.2 (*a*) Adding up particular election results: an even number of spaces between adjacent parties

Party A's vote = 500 + 600 + 600 + 800 + 600 + 900 = 4,000
Party B's vote = 1,000 + 900 + 1,000 + 1,100 = 4,000
NB: Calculations denominated in terms of 1,000 votes

79

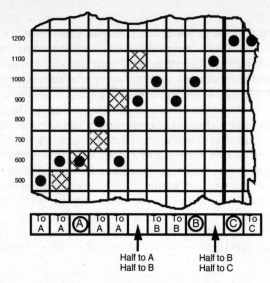

Fig. 6.2 (*b*) **Adding up particular election results: an odd number of spaces between adjacent parties**

Party A's vote = 500 + 600 + 600 + 800 + 600 + 900/2 = 3,500
Party B's vote = 900/2 + 1,000 + 900 + 1,000 + 1,100/2 = 3,900
NB: Calculations denominated in terms of 1,000 votes

board when the time-limit expires. The number of votes won by each party is decided as at rule 13. The numbers of votes won by each party at each election are then totalled, and the winner of the game is the party winning most votes overall during the game, or the only party left in the game if all other parties go bankrupt, or get bored and go home, before the game is over.

VARIATIONS ON A THEME

Party splits
If the game is played between teams, then players who are not party leaders may be allowed to split away from the main party and form a party of their very own. They do this simply by banging a

handy table, then making a defiant public announcement that they have ratted on their former party colleagues, telling the world about their new name and providing themselves with a distinctive playing piece to move around the board. Obviously, they get no cash. Defecting parties take their place in the sequence of moves immediately before the party they have just betrayed, on their first move placing their counter no more than two spaces away from the position of the party that loved, nurtured, and cared for them since political infancy.

Party fusions

Whether or not the game is played by teams, two parties at adjacent positions on the policy scale may be allowed to fuse into a single party. They do this by making a simple public announcement of their proposed union, speaking simultaneously while holding hands as they do so. GOD then recognizes their union as official, and no player may put asunder two parties that GOD has thus joined together. Parties that join together in this way then combine their campaign resources and take the policy position of the party with the greater number of votes. They do not combine their total of votes won before the fusion, however. The fused party takes the larger total of votes won to date by the two parties fusing, and the smaller party disposes of its playing-piece.

First-past-the-post elections

Instead of paying parties in proportion to how many votes they receive at the election, GOD gives the *entire pay-off of 200,000 to the party winning the most votes!* If two parties share this position, then GOD tosses a coin to decide which gets the entire pay-off. The winner of the game is the party that has come first in more elections than any other when the time-limit has elapsed. Astonishing and unrealistic as this variation might seem to the innocent bystander, this winner-takes-all voting system is in fact actually used for real elections in certain backward Western 'democracies' in which mass literacy has yet to have any significant impact on the political system.

More than one dimension of policy

This variation should only be attempted by intrepid gamesters, professional politicians, and/or confidence tricksters and even then a large bottle of navy rum is strongly recommended as an additional piece of equipment. Several election boards are used simultaneously to decide election results. Each board shows party support on a different dimension of policy. The number of weeks in the campaign is multiplied by the number of dimensions that are used. Thus a two-dimensional game requires two weeks of placing counters, followed by six weeks of campaigning. A three-dimensional game will need nine weeks. A 500-dimensional game, played simultaneously on 500 election boards, will need 1,500 weeks, and so on.

Players choose names for these dimensions and meanings for policy positions on each dimension by mutual agreement. Parties begin by in sequence placing a counter on the dimension of their choice. They then take turns to place a counter on a dimension that they have yet to stake a position on, and continue until they have staked a position on all dimensions. At this point all players who wish to do so take a large glass of navy rum. All rules of the game above apply, except that each week a party has the chance to shift position on one, and only one, policy dimension. Election results at the end of the campaign are determined by aggregating party support on each dimension.

Suggestions for extra policy dimensions are:

- *Moral policy.* This scale, which captures policy on social and moral conservatism, could measure the time-period that ought to elapse after the breakdown of a marriage before divorce is legally allowed. This could be divided into twenty un-even time-intervals spanning the time-period from zero to eternity.

- *Nationalism.* This scale, which measures the intensity of commitment to the national ideal, could measure the number of people it would be acceptable to kill in vindication of this. This could be divided into twenty uneven intervals spanning the range from zero to many millions. Equivalent scales could be constructed for religious or ethnic identity if these were felt more appropriate in particular circumstances.

• *Law and order.* This scale, which measures the extent to which parties promote hard-line policies on law and order, could measure the proposed penalty for a person convicted for a first offence of dealing in heroin. This could be denominated in prison sentences, and be divided into unequal periods spanning the range from zero to eternity.

The possibilities, of course, are endless.

COALITIONS

A game for between three and seven players/crews.

EQUIPMENT

A bundle of money, a pack of playing-cards from which all jokers and fives have been removed, a blackboard or sheet of paper to display the election results; a Trough (see Primitive Politics); a timer or day-and-night sound system (see Chapter 1).

RULES

1. The political system is controlled by the Game Overall Director (GOD) whose decisions on *every* matter are, as always, final.

2. Gangs of marauding politicians have banded together into political parties. Each political party is bargaining over getting into government and/or setting public policy on various important matters. One member of each party is identified as the leader. GOD allocates party names from the following list:

Hoodoos
Voodoos
Yahoos
Boogaloos
Pink Poodles
Chicken Noodles
Wang Dang Doodles

83

3. GOD gives each party a war chest of 200,000 at the beginning of time and political events unfold as follows.

4. GOD holds an election which decides each party's seat total in a 200-seat legislature by dealing cards from the bottom of the well-shuffled deck. First, the crew Bosses must pay to play. Each must pay 20,000 in 'election expenses' into an offshore bank account operated by GOD, who then deals a card to each party in turn until no more cards are left. Some parties may have one card fewer than others but that is just hard luck and GOD cares nothing about this—very little in politics is fair. The parties add up the face value of the cards in their hand. Aces are low while the aristocratic court cards, true to form, score zero points each.

5. After the first election has been held, GOD starts the music if a soundtrack is being used, after which the soundtrack just keeps running until the end of the game. If a soundtrack is not being used, GOD wakes everybody up and there is then a five-minute political night during which parties can do almost anything they like, including making deals with each other. Sometime during the night GOD, who of course has an infinite amount of money and to whom, therefore, any finite amount of money appears infinitesimal, tosses 200,000 nonchalantly into the Trough.

6. The parties must use the night to decide how to share the contents of the Trough between them.

7. After night comes day, two minutes of silence free from the sound of pounding rock music. During the day, the players can put proposals to GOD. If a group of parties feel they have reached an agreement, they write this on a piece of paper and give this as a proposal to GOD. A proposal must specify how the contents of the Trough are to be shared between political parties.

8. If more than one proposal is being thrust into GOD's open right hand at the same time, she has absolute discretion as to which of these to accept. As soon as she has accepted a proposal, GOD closes her right hand into a tight fist and puts this proposal to a vote, refusing to accept any other proposal until the vote has been taken.

9. Players can of course continue bargaining during the political day. But if a proposal is made to GOD during daylight hours, it will be put immediately to a vote and may be approved whether or not a particular player is paying attention.

10. Only party leaders are entitled to vote; any other player caught voting is punished and humiliated by GOD as she sees fit. If the total of seats controlled by parties voting for the proposal exceeds the total of seats controlled by parties voting against it, then the proposal is approved and it takes effect at once. Otherwise it fails, GOD opens her right hand again and is free to accept another proposal.

11. If a proposal is approved, then GOD scoops the contents out of the Trough, pays each party what has been approved and the round is over. Play resumes with another election as at rule 4.

12. Once three proposals have been made and defeated in a particular Round, however, GOD gets bored, the round is over and no pay-offs are made. The game resumes at rule 4 and people must pay again to play again.

13. Proposals can be neither made nor voted upon once political night has resumed. Players must wait for the next political day before making and voting upon further proposals. Any who might make some proposal to GOD in the middle of the night are treated with kindness and sympathy by the other players, but their actions have absolutely no effect whatsoever on the game.

14. The game ends when the soundtrack finishes or the agreed time-limit elapses. The party with the most money when this happens is the winner.

VARIATIONS

A. Setting a fiscal policy
The parties each have private preferences on the rate of income tax that should be levied. These are shown in Table 6.1.

The parties must settle on a tax rate. A proposal simply specifies this on a piece of paper placed in GOD's open right hand, as in rules 7–8. If it is approved, then GOD pays *each party*, regardless of whether or not the party was involved in the proposal, 200,000, minus 10,000 for every percentage point the approved tax rate differs from the party's preferred tax rate. If the proposed rate is more than 20 points adrift of the party's preferred rate, then the party must *pay* GOD 10,000 for every percentage point that the

Table 6.1

Party	Preferred rate of income tax (%)
Hoodoos	22
Voodoos	28
Yahoos	34
Boogaloos	40
Pink Poodles	46
Chicken Noodles	52
Wang Dang Doodles	58

deficit exceeds 20. Once three proposals have been made and defeated, GOD falls asleep, the round is over and no pay-offs are made.

B. Appointing a finance minister

As for Variation A except that, instead of proposing a tax rate directly, the players must select one party to control the finance ministry. A proposal specifies the party to control the finance ministry. If it is approved, then the specified party takes over the finance ministry and imposes its preferred tax rate. Pay-offs are the same as for Variation A.

C. Setting both a fiscal and a defence policy

The parties not only have private preferences on the rate of income tax that should be levied, but they are also concerned about what share of the taxes thus raised should be spent on national defence. Preferences on both issues are shown in Table 6.2. If there are only six parties in the game, then the Voodoos don't play; if there are only five parties, then omit both the Voodoos and the Wang Dang Doodles; if there are only four, then omit the Voodoos, the Yahoos, and the Wang Dang Doodles.

The parties must now decide on the shares of the budget to devote to guns and butter. A proposal specifies a share of the budget to be devoted to each. If it is approved, GOD pays each party 200,000, minus 10,000 for every percentage point the approved share differs from the party's preferred share for each area of public spending. If the proposed rate is more than 20 points adrift of the party's preferred rate, then the party must *pay* GOD 10,000 for

Table 6.2

Party	Income tax (%)	Budget share on defence (%)
Hoodoos	22	40
Voodoos	28	52
Yahoos	34	28
Boogaloos	40	58
Pink Poodles	46	22
Chicken Noodles	52	46
Wang Dang Doodles	58	34

every percentage point that the deficit exceeds 20. Once three proposals have been made and defeated, GOD becomes enraged, the round is over, and no pay-offs are made.

D. Appointing defence and social welfare ministers

As Variation C, except that instead of proposing shares of the budget devote to defence and social welfare directly, the players must select a party to control the defence ministry and a party to control the social welfare ministry—these may or may not be the same party. A proposal specifies the party to control each ministry. If it is approved the specified party takes over the defence ministry and imposes its preferred share of defence spending, while the specified party takes over the social welfare ministry and imposes its preferred share of social welfare spending. Pay-offs are as for Variation C.

E. Carving up a fixed prize *and* setting a finance policy

Combine Variation A and the basic game. A proposal must specify a tax rate and an allocation of 200,000 between parties. If the proposal passes, then each party gets its approved share of the 200,000, which may well be zero. Each party also gets 200,000, minus 10,000 for every percentage point the approved tax rate differs from the party's preferred tax rate, whether or not the party was involved in the proposal. If the proposed rate is more than 20 points adrift of the party's preferred rate, then the party must *pay* GOD 10,000 for every percentage point that the deficit exceeds 20. Once three proposals have been made and defeated, GOD goes into a trance, the round is over, and no pay-offs are made.

F. Carving up a fixed prize *and* appointing a finance minister

Combine Variation B and the basic game. A proposal must specify a party to control the finance ministry and an allocation of 200,000 between parties. Pay-offs as in Variation E.

G. Carving up a fixed prize *and* setting policy on guns and butter

Combine Variation C and the basic game. A large bottle of navy rum may be needed as additional equipment for this and the following variation. A proposal must specify shares of the budget devoted to defence and social welfare and an allocation of 200,000 between parties. If the proposal passes, each party gets its approved share of the 200,000, which may well be zero. Each party also gets 200,000, minus 10,000 for every percentage point the approved share differs from the party's preferred share for each area of public spending. If the proposed rate is more than 20 points adrift of the party's preferred rate, then the party must *pay* GOD 10,000 for every percentage point that the deficit exceeds 20. Once three proposals have been made and defeated, GOD drinks a large glass of navy rum, then puts her head in her hands. The round is over and no pay-offs are made.

H. Carving up a fixed prize *and* appointing defence and social welfare ministers

Combine Variation D and the basic game. A proposal must specify a party to control the defence and social welfare ministries—these may or may not be the same party—and an allocation of 200,000 between parties. Pay-offs as in Variation G.

I. Qualified majority voting

Combine the basic game or any of the above variations with a requirement that, instead of passing a proposal if more vote for than against it, a proposal is only passed if two-thirds of those voting support it.

COALECTIONS

A game for three to seven intrepid players/crews. This is a combination of the previous two games. The parties in Elections want only to get as many votes as possible, regardless of what might happen after the election. The parties in Coalitions want to squeeze as much as possible out of each coalition, regardless of what might happen at the next election. Coalections forces players to balance what happens in an election against the coalition bargaining that will follow, and to balance what happens in coalition bargaining with the consequences of this for the election that will inevitably come. Thus the game is similar to Coalitions; the main difference is that election results are determined by playing a game of Elections rather than dealing cards from the bottom of some dog-eared deck.

EQUIPMENT

Exactly the same equipment is used as for the game of Elections.

RULES

1. The game is set up in exactly the same way as for the game of Elections.

2. The election campaign and the election itself are conducted according to the rules for the game of Elections.

3. The election results are determined using a proportional representation system. For each 100,000 votes a party wins at the election, it receives 1 seat in parliament. Fractions of 100,000 votes go to lunatic-fringe parties which thankfully win no seats.

4. The total number of seats won by all parties taken together is calculated. The winning threshold is set at half this total, plus one, rounded down to the nearest seat. (Thus if the total of seats won is 195, the winning threshold is $195/2 + 1 = 98.5$, rounded down to 98 seats. If the number of seats won is 192, the winning threshold is $192/2 + 1 = 97$.)

5. Once the election results have been calculated, the winning threshold and the seat totals for each party are displayed prominently.

6. The parties must now form a winning coalition that can agree not only on how to divide up the contents of the Trough but also on a rate for income tax. In order to be successful, the coalition must therefore:

89

- control enough seats to equal or exceed the winning threshold;
- agree on how to divide up the contents of the Trough between players;
- agree on a level at which to set income tax.

7. The bargaining which precedes the formation of the coalition and the manner of making proposals take exactly the same form as in the game of Coalitions. A proposal for a government must specify a tax rate and an allocation of 200,000 between parties.

8. Each party's policy on income tax is the policy that is indicated by its position on the Elections board. If the proposal passes, each party gets its approved share of the 200,000 in the Trough, which may well be zero. Each party *in the coalition* also gets 200,000, minus 10,000 for every percentage point the approved tax rate differs from the party's ideal tax rate, whether or not the party was involved in the proposal. Once three proposals have been made and defeated, the round is over, no pay-offs are made, and another election is held.

9. Once the coalition has formed, there is another election, as in rules 2–5 above.

10. The winner is the party with most money at the end of the game.

VARIATIONS

Any combination of the variations described for the games of Elections and Coalitions can be used.

7 Playing Party Games

PLAYING AT ELECTIONS

Players will soon discover that the opening declaration of party policy is a vital part of the game. Recovering from a bad opening position by subsequently changing party policy costs scarce campaign funds. The more campaign funds that must be used at this early stage to do this, the less will be available later in the game for winning elections.

Having the first move in this context is quite definitely *not* an advantage, since parties forced to declare their policies early are more likely to be outflanked. Parties moving later can do the outflanking. Thus early-moving parties must think very hard indeed about the response of other parties to the positions that they stake out for themselves.

By far the most zombie-voters, who typically shy away in ill-disguised horror from extreme policy positions of any stripe, are to be found in the middle of the policy scale. This means that parties may well be tempted to rush in and stake their ideological claims in this fertile middle ground. But they should never forget that the others will also think the same way. It's no good whatsoever wallowing blissfully in the middle of a huge pile of votes only to find out all too soon that several rival parties are snuggled up on either side of you.

A party declaring its policy relatively late in the day will have a lot more to go on. The really wide open spaces will already have been taken, of course, but the remaining parties may well be able to spot some lucrative gaps in the market, positions where there is at least a medium-sized pile of voters to whom no one is currently appealing.

Parties should also consider staking out a position at one end or the other of the policy scale. There are fewer votes to be won there overall, to be sure, but this is offset not only by the presence of fewer rivals but also by the big advantage (particularly when the swing goes their way) that the extreme parties will scoop all votes on the far-flung sides of their positions. If the swing does go in their favour, then they'll already be where they want to be and won't have to spend campaign funds getting there. If the swing goes the other way, then their losses may be at least partially offset if rival parties try to follow the movement of votes, freeing up potential support on the less popular side of the policy scale. In all circumstances the most important thing to do is to avoid being boxed in by parties on either side who take up very similar policies to your own. To get out of this trap will cost money or lose votes.

Once the first opinion poll has been held, everyone will have some idea of the likely result of the next election. Once they have seen which way the wind is blowing, they may want to change policy to take account of likely election results. But remember that any significant change in policy position costs money as the party making the move has to explain what is going on, and why, to the electorate. The swing may change again in the short term, and it will almost certainly change in the longer term, in which event moving back to where you started on the policy scale will not only make you look stupid but will cost still more campaign funds to pull off.

As the weeks pass and the next election approaches, the incentives for parties to move will increase. The swing in the next election will at some stage become a foregone conclusion—it will always be known for sure in the final week of the campaign. This means that the incentive to change direction once again on policy, spending scarce campaign funds in the process, will disappear.

The last week of the campaign may well present parties with their hardest decisions. They'll have more information than at any other stage of the campaign, and there's less chance of being out-manoeuvred. Especially the last-moving parties will be tempted to make a large and expensive move into the middle of the biggest unclaimed pile of votes, unless they're lucky or skilful enough to be there already. However, the vagaries and random elements in the election results can still upset everything. Parties may therefore decide to play it safe, staying put in the hope that next time the swing will come back in their direction, saving their thunder and campaign funds for another day when these might be more effective.

In general there are thus two basic styles of campaigning that a party can adopt. One is to keep in continual touch with movements in electoral opinion, modifying policies all the time so as to increase the chance of winning the current election. Hopping frantically about in this way will be expensive and raises the risk of running right out of money, leaving the party floating helplessly in policy space, at the mercy of its rivals in the crucial final stages of some campaign. At the end of the day, however, money means nothing in itself to a party leader—who only wants campaign funds to win votes and gains nothing at all from having money in the bank after the last election has been fought and the voters are all tucked safely up in their beds. Indeed a party leader who has anything at all left in the bank at the end of the game has almost certainly missed some opportunity for winning more votes, and deserves vilification rather than praise.

The alternative style of campaigning is for a party to stay put like a pudding and save its campaign funds, waiting for shifts in opinion to swing voters back in its favour. The benefit in doing this lies in keeping a healthy stock of campaign funds that might help the party to leap out of some nasty corner that it might one day find itself in, or into some tasty space that might open up at a later stage in the game. But proponents of the pudding strategy should not forget the admonition in the previous paragraph about the usefulness of left-over campaign funds—these are of no use whatsoever to person or beast and represent a missed opportunity to any ambitious politician.

The decision on which style to play is partly a matter of personal taste: some people are natural puddings while other are hoppers at heart, but it also depends on what the other parties are doing. If you do well at elections by frolicking extravagantly around all over the place, you may win more campaign funds to help you frolic even more extravagantly in the future. The pudding strategy may conserve campaign funds for later, but party leaders of this persuasion must not let the others get too far ahead of them. If they do this, then blowing their entire war chest to parachute the pudding into some magnificent open ideological space late in the game may not reap enough votes to make up for lost ground.

Moving beyond things that parties can do on their own, collusion between two or more parties can also be very effective. As always, the possibility of side payments between players opens up interesting possibilities. This is party politics after all, in which anything goes, and it is quite legitimate to reward one of the other parties for not making a particular move, or for attacking a dangerous opponent. Side payments also open up intriguing new sources of income for those who think that they will do badly in a particular election. Such parties can try to place themselves in an ideological position in which they are worth paying off by others, or worth employing by some party to do a particular piece of dirty work.

One collusive strategy that works well is for two adjacent parties to agree to move slowly apart. They should not leave so large a gap between them that it becomes worth while for some rich rival to pay up and hop into the middle, but they should move far enough apart to ensure that a tasty portion of zombie-voters can be carved up between them. Whether colluding with some other party or playing alone, however, the real key to this game is never to forget what the other players can do in response to the superficially brilliant moves that you might make.

PLAYING THE ELECTION VARIATIONS

Party splits

More intriguing and mischievous options open up once party splits are allowed. One especially sneaky possibility is for a party to pretend to split, but then go on to collude with the breakaway faction or factions. This enables a party to 'spread' itself further across the board. Instead of occupying a single point on the policy scale, it will now occupy two or more points. If the positions of the breakaway factions are chosen carefully, so as not to allow enough space between the faction and the main party to be interesting to some carpet-bagging opportunist, then the party can use its breakaway factions to protect itself from attack by rivals. In the closing stages of the game, the breakaway factions could then recombine with the main party (if it will have them back), offering up some juicy piles of zombie-voters for exploitation, in exchange for a share of the final loot.

There is also, of course, the likelihood of hostile splits. A faction may spot a gap in the market that has been missed by the party leadership and, rather than point it out for the good of the party as a whole, jump ship and take advantage of the gap as a breakaway faction. This is not likely to happen towards the end of the game unless the breakaway faction anticipates subsequently joining any other party or has simply got fed up to the back teeth with some tiresome party leader and feels like lashing out. But splitting away from the main party towards the beginning of the game may offer a faction some intriguing possibilities. It will be necessary to jump ship at a time when there is some reasonable chance of doing well at the next election, because only then can campaign resources be earned for future rounds.

Party fusions
Since two fusing parties can't combine their cumulative vote harvest but must make do with the vote harvest of the larger, the incentives for fusion are as limited in the game as they are in the real world. But they do exist, especially in later stages of the game. A party that has next to no chance of winning may find itself (or indeed might put itself) close to a party that has a decent chance of winning. In the final election of the game, the smaller party could fuse with the larger, removing its counter from the board and in effect turning over at least a share of its supporters to the larger. Obviously the smaller party would expect some share of the final pay-off in exchange for doing this. Fusing early in the game seems to have little logic, however, as the other parties will quickly be able to move to take advantage of the fact that there is now only one counter on the board where before there were two.

First-past-the-post elections
If the first-past-the-post variation is used, then all pay-offs after each election go only to the largest party. It will be dangerous to let any one party win too many elections in a row since, quite apart from racking up election wins that will help it to win the overall game, the winning party will be awash with campaign funds and better placed to fight future elections.

The net effect of this should be that parties attempt more dramatic policy shifts under the first-past-the-post system, especially late in each campaign, since there is a high premium on hitting just the right spot to beat all others. In the basic game, which uses proportional representation, all parties receive some pay-off after each election, both in campaign funds and in votes that count towards the final score, so precise policy positions are less critical. Coming a close second is almost as good as coming first. Under first-part-the-post rules, in contrast, coming a close second is no better than coming last, so that the closing stages of each election should be volatile and hectic.

The choice of electoral system has an interesting interaction with the possibility of party splits and fusions. The incentives to split are much less with the first-past-the-post system, since the breakaway faction will win nothing at all unless it can somehow get to be the largest party. The only incentive to split, apart from the unlikely possibility of splitting away to become the election winner, is the possibility of splitting to join a more successful party. Conversely, the attractiveness of party fusions is enhanced by first-past-the-post rules, precisely because there is such a premium on being the largest party.

More than one dimension of policy

I must (or rather I will) be honest and confess that I have never played this game with more than one dimension of policy, nor have I heard of anyone else who has done so. I would, however, love to find a band of intrepid gamesters to try it out. The multi-dimensional version is thus a fantasy rather than a reality, and is almost certainly going to be easier to manage and play if someone programs it for a personal computer. There have been those in the past who have offered to do so, but sadly they have all fallen by the wayside for one reason or another.

In theory, the extra dimensions should add at least two layers of complexity to the strategic calculations needed, given the need to trade off the benefits of spending campaign funds on one dimension rather than another, and the problem of deciding a sequence of moves on different dimensions to achieve the desired effect. As with all games in which real blood has yet to be spilt, however, all sorts of other surprising effects will no doubt pop up and a wide variety of disasters are waiting to happen.

Overall

Overall, taking the basic game and its variations together, the key skills needed to win are a good spatial sense of where the main gaps in the market are to be found, and the ability to look forward and anticipate the reactions of rivals. Those who lose the game tend to do so by leaping too soon into what may seem to the short-sighted to be attractive vote-winning positions, only to find themselves being boxed in towards the closing stages of a campaign by rivals who have moved to shut down any threat to their own position.

PLAYING AT COALITIONS

You'll notice a strong smell of Primitive Politics when playing Coalitions. You'll see a clear need to co-operate with other parties, without which no government can be formed and no prizes won. Yet at the end of the day you'll know there is only one winner, so that all parties are in fundamental conflict with one another. Playing Coalitions forces people to balance these mixed motives. While each party wants to make as much as possible for itself, each must also offer enough to the others to ensure that they want to do business with it.

There will always be quite a few different winning coalitions for any given election result. You'll do well to rule some of these out straight away. For example, you won't gain anything by letting into a winning coalition any party whose votes aren't absolutely essential to a majority. Such parties are passengers. Since they add nothing to the ability of the coalition to win, why take them along for the ride and give them a share of the pay-off? Once you rule out all coalitions that carry passengers, each of the remaining coalition partners you will be looking at will be 'pivotal', in the sense that if any one of them leaves, then this will turn a winning coalition into a losing one. Every pivotal player, indeed, can leave a winning coalition and join the coalition of all other players to make another winning coalition. This power is the basis of the threats that potential coalition partners make to each other as they try to do the best deal for themselves. The more a party finds itself pivotal in different coalitions, the more threats it can make and the more powerful it is.

In the basic game, this means that the bargaining is likely to be chaotic and unstable. Imagine you're doing a deal to form a three-party coalition that carries no passengers and controls a majority of the seats. Since each of the three parties is equally pivotal to the success or failure of this coalition, no matter how many seats it has, you might agree with the other parties to split the prize into three equal parts. But imagine there are two other parties in the game who will get nothing at all as things stand. You (or either of your two coalition partners for that matter) could approach the outsiders and offer to let them stick their noses in the Trough if they each take only a tiny taste, say 20,000 or so to cover their expenses which is of course better than nothing, and leave you with the remaining 160,000. Of course another member of the original coalition, who is now in danger of being chased away from the Trough entirely, could beat that by offering the two outsiders 40,000 each and taking a mere 120,000 for herself. You, or someone else, could counter this by offering the 'outsiders' (who are by now not doing so very badly) 60,000 each and taking 80,000 for yourself. This process of offer and counter-offer can go on and on; there's no natural stopping point. Every offer that can be made can be bettered. This means that bargaining would go on and on until the players died of exhaustion or frustration if there was nothing to stop it. In practice of course, some chance factor that has nothing much to do with the game—the fact that two of the players are in love with each other, for example, or mad—will probably intervene and pick out one deal rather than another as the one that is used to share out the contents of the Trough.

As you play the game you'll quickly find out that the relationship between the number of seats you win at each election and your subsequent bargaining power is much less obvious than it seems at first sight. Bargaining power, as we have already seen, is based upon the ability to make threats and in this game the threats you can make are threats to leave and join other coalitions. So your bargaining power is closely related to the number of coalitions of which you're a pivotal member. The more coalitions you can smash up by leaving, the stronger you are.

This power can change very erratically. Imagine for example to keep things simple, a game played between three parties and an election in which each wins about the same number of seats. It's not hard to see that they will all be equally powerful. None will be able to form a winning coalition alone, yet each will be able to form one in partnership with either of the other parties. Each will have the same number of threats to make, and therefore the same amount of bargaining power. Suppose one party does very badly at the next election, losing support equally to its two rivals. Even a disastrous electoral performance, however, might leave it no worse off *in terms of bargaining power*. Say the losing party ends up with only ten of 200 seats, while the other two parties have 95 seats each. As a matter of fact, the bargaining power of the 'losing' party is unchanged. It still takes two parties to form a winning coalition and any two of them will do. There is no reason, therefore, why the smaller party should take a smaller share of the pay-off than before. It is just as pivotal as ever to any coalition that might form. There is still only one winning coalition which works without it, and two that need its support. If I was the leader of a small party that found itself in this position, then I'd demand an equal share of the pay-off. There would be much weeping and wailing about the 'unfairness' of a much smaller party getting the same share of the Trough as a much larger one, but that wouldn't faze me one little bit. I'd simply ask the wailers to show me where it says anything *whatsoever* about being 'fair' in the *Big Book of Politics*.

On the other hand, very small changes in seat share can have quite very big effects on bargaining power. Imagine a game played between four parties. At one election each party has 50 seats and obviously each has the same amount of bargaining power. At the next election you lose two seats, one each to two of the other parties. This leaves you with 48 seats, and the other three with 51, 51, and 50 respectively. Those two lost seats have cost you a huge amount of bargaining power. In fact you now have no bargaining power at all, since you are a passenger in any coalition that might form. Any two of the other parties can form a winning coalition of at least 101 seats. And any winning coalition that you belong to would still be winning if you left, so you do not have anything at all with which to threaten the others. You can try, but I'm sorry to say they will just pat you on the head and tell you to run away and play in the traffic. Winning the two seats back again, of course, would result in a huge increase in your bargaining power.

Thus, while you can win or lose a lot of seats and end up with the same bargaining power, you can also win or lose a very small number of seats and either gain or lose a very large amount of bargaining power. Worse, you can win seats and lose power. Imagine you're the first of four parties that win 40, 40, 40, and 80 seats at one election, respectively, then go on in a second election to share the seats 44 to you, and 52 seats to each of the others. You've won seats, but in the process become quite irrelevant to coalition formation. Whereas before you were the pivotal member of quite a few winning coalitions, now you are pivotal in absolutely none. Work it out for yourself if you don't believe me.

PLAYING THE COALITION VARIATIONS

Setting a fiscal policy or appointing a finance minister

You won't play these first variations for long because they're so easy to crack. The parties are arranged along a scale of policy just like the one in Elections (above). The election result will decide which party is sitting right in the centre of the game, at the median position, in the sense that if you add the seat totals from either end of the scale, then adding this party's seats into the total makes the difference between winning and losing. This 'median' party really is in the catbird seat in all coalition negotiations. Actually, it can insist on setting policy at its ideal position. A coalition of parties controlling a majority of seats will vote against anything to the left of this; another majority coalition will vote against anything to the right of it. The ideal policy position of the median party can beat any other policy position in a majority vote and should therefore prevail against any alternative that is proposed. The players can do no better than to propose the ideal policy position of the median party or to propose the median party as the one to control the finance ministry, which has the same effect. The game is thus degenerate, in the sense that the outcome is in effect decided by the election result that determines which party sits in this glorious position. It's actually a game of chance, assuming the players are not completely stupid.

Setting policy on guns *and* butter

In contrast to the degenerate simplicity that prevails when only one dimension of policy has to be settled, all hell breaks loose when more than one dimension is considered at the same time. Just as in the basic game where the contents of a simple Trough of money are shared out, there is typically no 'natural' solution for the players to settle upon in this variation. As a result, any deal that can be made can be bettered by some other deal that will find the support of a majority. Once more, since any deal done can be bettered, the outcome is likely to be settled by chance factors that have nothing to do with the game, though this will do nothing to dampen the ferocity of bargaining between serious game players.

Appointing ministers of defence and welfare

In contrast to the previous variation, setting policy on two dimensions at the same time by appointing ministers who are allowed to implement their ideal policy does allow for certain stable outcomes if only the players can find them! Infuriatingly for the players, sometimes there is no stable solution to their problem, sometimes there is just one solution, and sometimes there is more than one solution. It is quite often the case that one of the parties, not necessarily the largest, will find itself in a particularly strong bargaining position and will be able to get away with insisting on taking both cabinet portfolios for itself, while no majority coalition of the other parties can agree on anything that they prefer to this. Of course it is easy for party leaders to strut around pretending to be in this position, but they will very often find that if they do this, then they can be sidelined by some coalition of their rivals. But quite often in this game a shrewd party leader may actually turn out to be right in the heart of the action, with no effective response available to her rivals.

Carving up a fixed prize *and* setting a policy position

Now things start to get *really* tricky, of course, since parties will be trading off pay-offs from the Trough against pay-offs that they get from the policy positions set by the winning coalition. It's no longer clear that the party in the median policy position is in the catbird seat in such negotiations, since the two sources of a party's bargaining power, its policy position and the number of winning coalitions in which it is arithmetically pivotal, will interact in tantalizing and infuriating ways. It's in this sort of game that actually getting a feel for how the bargaining might pan out will be of far more use than all the theories in the world.

Qualified majority voting

Players should quickly figure that the need for a qualified majority of, let's say, two-thirds of all seats can make it possible for no winning coalition to form, raising the serious possibility of deadlock. This is because the need for a qualified majority implies the empowerment of a blocking minority. When two-thirds plus one of the votes are needed to win, for example, then any actor or coalition controlling one-third of the votes can block any victory. Quite unlike the situation with simple majority decision-making, there can be more than one blocking minority in existence at the same time, and these may want completely incompatible things. There may be more than one 'median' party, and the outcome of political bargaining may have much more to do with the ability to face down other parties than with anything else.

To see this imagine the game that under majority rule was degenerate, the game in which the parties had to agree a position on one dimension of policy before they could form a winning coalition. Imagine five parties, A, B, C, D, E arranged from left to right on fiscal policy, each winning forty of the 200 seats in some election, as shown in Fig. 7.1. With two-thirds majority rule, 134 seats are needed to win.

This means that four parties must combine to form a winning coalition and consequently that any two parties can block any proposal. This in turn has the effect that, any proposal to move rightwards from the ideal position of Party B will be blocked by Parties A and B, while any proposal to move leftwards from this position will be blocked by every party except A. Any proposal to move leftwards from the ideal position of Party D will be blocked by Parties D and E, while any proposal to move rightwards from this position will be blocked by every party except E. And a move from any position between the ideal positions of Parties B and D will be blocked by the two or more parties on the opposite side of the direction of the proposed move.

Even a proposed move from some 'extreme' position, such as Party A's ideal policy position, will be controversial. Since the parties will figure out quickly that, once they opt for a position in between B and D, any move away from this will be blocked, they will find it almost impossible to agree where to move to, even if four of them agree that a move from Party A's unpopular ideal

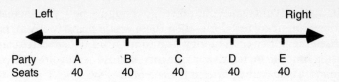

Fig. 7.1   Five parties on one dimension of policy

Qualified majority needed = 134 seats

position would make them all better off. They may thus even find themselves stuck at Party A's extreme position because they are in head-to-head confrontation about where to go from there.

The shift from a simple to a qualified majority will thus make a big, big difference to the conduct of the game. Once more, rolling up your sleeves and getting down to bargaining in the game will give you a much better feel for what is going on than rather abstract theories, which are not currently very useful in interpreting the dynamics of qualified majority rule.

PLAYING COALECTIONS

Many of the tricks described in the previous two chapters can be brought to bear on Coalections. There are, however, some very important differences to keep firmly in mind.

Consider the election campaign first. When playing Elections the aim of each party is to get as many votes as possible. Whichever electoral system is used, getting more votes increases the chances of winning. In Coalections the pay-off is not made automatically to any party. Even the largest party may well end up with nothing if enough of the others gang up against it. Parties are therefore fighting elections in order to increase their bargaining power in subsequent coalition negotiations.

We have already seen that this bargaining power increases in rather peculiar ways. While you can never make yourself worse off by winning more seats, everything else being equal, you may well end up no better off. And you may even be worse off if support for the other parties changes in ways that are unhelpful to you. On the other hand, sometimes winning just a few more seats can dramatically increase your power. If changing policy to increase your support cost nothing, then there would be no problem, but changing policy costs money. You won't want to use scarce campaign funds to increase your vote total if those extra votes give you no more bargaining power at the end of the day.

It's not that simple, however, since small policy changes, costing relatively little, can reap even richer returns in bargaining power than they do in votes. Consider the examples used in the previous chapter. If there are three parties, all with about the same number of votes, then you must improve your election results spectacularly to get any more power. In fact you have to do so well that you end up with more than half of the seats all on your own. In these circumstances you might not feel at all inclined to spend money on attracting more votes unless you thought that you could do just that. Anything else would just be money down the drain. You'd get more votes, but so what?

If there are four parties, however, and the other three have just over fifty seats each while you have just under fifty seats, then you'll be left out of any coalition as an irrelevant passenger if you do nothing about it. Even a very small vote gain may well put you right back in the action. Instead of having to win the thirty-odd extra seats needed in the previous example before your power goes up, a mere two or three extra seats might be enough to produce a massive improvement in your bargaining position. In this case any campaign funds spent on getting those vital extra seats would be very well spent indeed.

If only things were that simple! But winning extra votes at Coalections may well mean changing party policy. As well as costing you campaign funds in the election, changing your policy will affect the pay-off you get if you do get into a coalition. This is because you pay a penalty if you go into a coalition with a policy that is different from the policy your own party was peddling so publicly at the end of the most recent election. What is more, your policy affects your attractiveness to other likely coalition partners. The closer your policy to theirs, the more likely it is that they will want to form a coalition with you. In this way, your policy affects your bargaining power as well as your arithmetical pay-off.

All of this means that there are several more reasons that might make you change policy during the election campaign, over and above simplistic calculations about how many votes you expect to win. You might change your own policy to make it is closer to the policies of other parties because this makes you a more attractive coalition partner and in this way makes you more powerful. You will, if you are any good at all at this business, have some idea about which coalitions are likely to form and which policy each is likely to decide upon; using these estimates, you may try to get as close to the policy of some expected coalition as possible so that, if you do get into a coalition you'll have to pay as small a penalty as possible for having a party policy that differs from coalition policy.

Changing your policy has clearly become quite a complicated decision! To sum up, there are four main factors you must consider, and any move you make will often help you with some of these and harm you with others. Actually working out the costs and benefits of a particular move becomes extremely complicated, given all of the uncertainties involved. You really will have to begin to play by 'feel' rather than trying to function like a human calculator.

The main effects of a change in your tax policy are:

- it may increase your seat share but cost you money in scarce campaign funds that might be better used later in the game (this is the standard dilemma in Elections);
- even if you increase your seat share, you may or may not increase your bargaining power;
- it may affect your pay-off if you get into a coalition; it might be worth making a 'free' move of one policy position to achieve this;
- it may affect your attractiveness as a coalition partner, which affects your chances of sharing in any pay-off at all.

It is quite possible that a particular change in policy may increase your seats and bargaining power, but move you further away from likely coalition partners. This would make you less attractive to others, and cost you more money in penalties if you succeed in getting into government. On the other hand, it is equally possible that a move which loses you votes might be a good one, because it does not damage your bargaining power very much, yet makes you a more attractive coalition partner. Despite the fact that you have fewer seats, you might be more likely to get into the government as a result of a particular change of policy. In Coalections, small can be beautiful if what you say sounds good to the others.

The other major difference between Coalections and the previous party games is the type of deal that you might make with others. In the first place, deals are now much more likely. Parties will want to co-ordinate their policies to get the most out of being in government, yet will want to make sure that opponents do not capitalize on this. As far as coalitions are concerned, parties should ideally place themselves right next to each other on the policy scale, so that they pay very few penalties if they go into government. This, however, will mean that the next election will be open season for parties that are not in the government to roam wild and free around different policies and capture large numbers of government votes. In contrast, election deals usually involve parties agreeing to keep their distance from other partners in crime, with one agreeing not to encroach upon the other's support as long as the other returns the favour. This type of deal can be rather expensive when it comes to forming a coalition, however, since coalitions between parties with rather different policy positions pay more in penalties than coalitions between parties with more similar policies.

Opposition parties will be faced with a similar set of dilemmas. If the government parties huddle together with similar tax policies, then there will be a temptation to rampage around the board at election time, scooping up votes as if they are going out of fashion. Every party's objective, however, is to get into government, since this is the only way to get a pay-off. Rampaging around the policy arena might be all very well at election time, but there will be a price to pay when it comes to forming a government. This increases the incentives for opposition parties to do deals with each other. If they don't co-operate, then they'll also be hampered in their campaign to attract votes from the government parties by the fact that they are in competition with each other. If opposition parties can come to some arrangement, then they can try to huddle together themselves, and co-ordinate an election campaign which wins votes but does not leave them paying heavy penalties when it comes to forming a government. If the government parties are sitting astride the centre of the policy spectrum, however, which is what coalition governments often tend to do, then there will be much less opportunity for a group of opposition parties, some of which are to the left, and some to the right, of the government, to do any serious huddling.

Another alternative wheeze for the opposition parties is to try to seduce some member of the current coalition by promising very favourable terms after the next election. As you will have seen from playing Coalitions, attempted seductions of this sort can quickly result in chaos, setting off a flurry of bids and counterbids. This might be just what some mischievous member of the opposition wants, figuring that discombobulating the current coalition by seducing one of its members is a fun alternative to slugging it out at the next election.

8 Real Party Games

REAL ELECTIONS

Whether or not you find the game of Elections to be realistic will depend on what you think of its core assumption. This is that politicians are concerned above all else to maximize votes and will offer voters—who in the real world are of course living, loving, and laughing non-zombies—whatever policies are needed to achieve this. This is not quite as cynical as it might sound the first time you hear it, since it does allow for the possibility that politicians see themselves as having a sacred duty to represent the wishes of voters, changing policies when these wishes change and measuring their success at doing this by how many votes they win. On this account, the urge to maximize votes boils down to an urge on the part of politicians to serve the public as best they can. It must be said, however, that the game will probably have a special appeal to those cynics who see politicians as people who just lust after power and will say whatever it takes in order to get this. Thus the game assumes that politicians are trying to maximize their votes by producing the most popular policies, either because they feel this to be their public duty or because they crave the private rewards that flow from this. We can draw a discreet veil over the real source of this motivation.

Elections also assume that politicians know something about the views of the electorate and about how these change over time. The basic game simplifies matters by dealing only with one issue—the level of income tax. This issue spreads the parties along a traditional left–right dimension that is one of the most familiar ways of describing politics in modern political systems. The one-dimensional version of Elections is quite unashamedly based upon a theory of party competition set out in one of the most famous books in political science, *An Economic Theory of Democracy* by Anthony Downs. Like all truly influential books, this one is rarely read but often referred to; most people prefer to rely upon commentaries. One such commentary can be found in my *Private Desires, Political Action*, another in a recent and excellent introduction to the field, *Analysing Politics* by Kenneth Shepsle and Stephen Bonchek.

Many important political issues array parties along the left–right ideological dimension and these can be substituted for the examples I have just given if it makes literal-minded players feel that the game is more realistic. Examples of such issues include: the share of national income that should be devoted to public expenditure; the proportion of business and industry that should be held in public ownership; the level of subsidization of various state-financed public services; the extent to which the State should get involved in redistributing income from rich to poor; and so on.

Many important political issues cut across this dimension. Recent examples include: foreign policy; policy on moral issues such as abortion and euthanasia; immigration policy; policy towards ethnic and other minorities; and so on. It is obviously a gross oversimplification of reality to represent all policy positions that might be offered to voters at election time as if they can be placed at one particular point on a single left–right scale. Hard-core game junkies can try to make the game more realistic, as suggested in one of the variations, by playing it simultaneously on a number of different boards, each representing an important dimension of policy.

Ordinary sane people, however, both in the game of Elections and the real thing, will most likely reduce the complexity of the decisions they face by behaving as if the campaign is fought out between politicians concerned to maximize their votes by optimizing their policy position on a single left–right scale. This means that a lot of parties will want to be in the same place—the middle. If the election is fought by only two parties, indeed, they should end up very close to each other in the centre of the board, more or less regardless of the distribution of voters. Some people claim that real two-party systems often look like this, the key players take up middle-of-the-road positions that are rather hard to tell apart, at least if they want to win elections. One explanation is that, with no other rivals to worry about, parties can neglect more extreme voters and move steadily towards each other. Voters on the extremes will vote for them anyway, however grumpy they might feel about this, since this is the best that they can do. The place where votes are to be won is the centre, where they can be snatched by one party from the grasp of its opponent.

Of course, in the real world (wherever *that* might be) we find almost no true two-party systems. The USA probably comes closest, but even their recent Presidential elections have tended to throw up third-party challengers. Add another party to the mix and the pattern changes drastically. Everyone still heads for the centre, but it becomes really bad news to be caught in the middle. If this happens to you, your two opponents grab the votes on either side of you, leaving for you only those voters who are really, really close to your own position. Of course you can try hopping out of this clinch and putting one of your rivals in the middle. But then they will do the same thing, putting you back where you started. It all looks very unstable. Even if there is no change at all in the views of the voters, each party will spend each election campaign hopping frantically about in an attempt not to be squeezed between its two closest rivals when the music stops and the votes are finally counted. Perhaps this instability is why three-party systems are about as common in the real world of politics as three-legged politicians.

If there are more than three parties, then the scramble for the centre can become much less important. Parties may spread themselves out across the policy scale and stay there. Working in from the extremes of the policy scale, the parties that are furthest to the left or right should move towards the centre until they are up against their closest rival. This rival has little incentive to move towards the centre, since it will only be chased in by the more extreme party, thereby losing more votes than it gains. Leaving aside shifts in public opinion, therefore, there may well be stable configurations of party policy positions when more than three parties fight an election.

Real party politics does not consist of endless changes of party policy in an attempt to adapt to every slight shift in public opinion or move by a rival party. At least two things stop parties from charging around all over the place. These are the cost of changing policies and the uncertainties involved in working out the best policy for winning votes, given the policies of rival parties. The higher the cost and the greater the uncertainty, the less likely a change of party policy. The costs to a party of changing its policies include the costs of campaigning to tell voters what has happened, and even sometimes why it has happened. They also include any loss of credibility that a party might suffer each time it makes a big policy shift. Other parties are not slow to spot broken promises and crow over these, while voters start losing track of what a party really stands for if its policy changes too often. What is more, in a changing world there is always the chance that public opinion will swing back in a party's favour. This will allow it to reap the benefit of votes shifting its way, as well as cashing in on the shift by boasting about what might even look to innocent bystanders like honesty and commitment to principles. The more uncertain the world is, the greater the chance that a party will end up with votes swinging in its favour by pure chance, and the less inclined it will be to waste resources and credibility on changing policies and telling voters about this.

One of the things which the game gives players a chance to do is to play around with different voting systems and explore the effect that these might have on the range of policies put forward by the parties. The first-past-the-post voting system, used in Britain and many former British colonies such as the USA, encourages parties to combine into larger and larger units and punishes party splits, both in the game and in reality. This is because the electoral system gives all of the goodies to the party with more votes than any other. The logical conclusion of this process is the emergence of two large parties confronting each other in the centre of the policy scale with roughly equal strength. While this process can rarely been seen playing out to its degenerate conclusion in the real world, it is none the less true that the first-past-the-post system does tend drastically to reduce the number of parties in the fight. Very few parties that split away from one of the big ones can survive in a first-past-the-post system, with the result that smart politicians almost never split away in the first place. Conversely, the benefits of joining a larger rather than a smaller party can be considerable. In short, first-past-the-post systems tend to have a small number of largish parties putting forward policies that are rather similar to each other and close to the centre of the policy scale.

Proportional representation, the electoral system used in the basic game, tends to have the opposite effect. This voting system encourages parties to split, since two 'smaller' parties can cover more ideological ground, and hence appeal to more voters, than one larger party. Proportional representation, for the same reason, provides parties with few benefits if they combine. Thus the number of parties in the system tends to be large. Furthermore, proportional representation tends not to reward parties that go hunting for votes at any cost. Each party has some chance of getting in on the action as long as it wins some votes. For these reasons proportional representation systems encourage the set parties taken together to offer a wider range of policies to voters, while party policies tend to change less dramatically from election to election.

Overall, and whatever electoral system is used, the basic way to win elections both in the game and in reality is to look for gaps in the market and fill these. Gaps in the electoral market manifest themselves as groups of voters to which no party is appealing. Of course, unless there is a party for every distinctive group of voters, there will always some voters who have to settle for second best when it comes to deciding which party to support at election time. This is because it only makes sense for a party to make a move to fill some gap in the market if it wins more votes than it loses as a result. This trade-off is what drives party strategy at elections, whether these are spelt with a large or a small 'e'.

REAL COALITIONS

While it might seem a weird and wonderful way of doing things to those more familiar with Britain or the USA, most of the really successful European economies have been run by coalition governments for most of the post-war era. Coalition government, therefore, is very much the norm in modern parliamentary democracies. Even Japan, long-cited as a classic example of a country with a strong tradition of one-party governments, has moved into an era of coalition cabinets after the breakaway of certain key factions from the formerly dominant Liberal Democratic Party.

Government coalitions must typically agree on two important matters before they are in a position to take over the reins of power. These are the distribution of cabinet portfolios between coalition members, and the precise policies to be adopted by the coalition government on the major policy issues that are likely to arise during the lifetime of the government.

In the basic game, the cabinet is seen in terms of a Trough, containing a fixed prize that is awarded to members of the successful coalition if they can agree upon how to share this out. The fact that the prize is fixed represents one particular way of looking at the rewards of forming a coalition government. According to this approach, the rewards of office are seen as a given set of trophies to be shared out between the winners, and each of these trophies is valued more or less for its own sake. Parties are in effect assumed to be driven solely by the desire to get into office so as to be able to stick their noses into the Trough. The best examples of such trophies are seats at the cabinet table—which are often viewed as the things that motivate politicians to fight as hard as they can to get into government, whether at elections, or in the coalition bargaining that follows. A position in the cabinet is often seen as the crowning glory of a political career, something to be valued more or less in and for itself.

If the desire to take control of a fixed set of trophies such as cabinet seats is indeed what motivates politicians, then this implies that winning coalitions will not tend to include parties whose seats are not essential to the survival of the government. Such 'surplus' parties will be seen as passengers—consuming some of the valuable contents of the Trough while contributing nothing to the ability of the coalition as a whole to capture these. And, in reality, it is indeed true that quite a few of the governments that do form are 'minimal winning' coalitions—coalitions that carry no passengers in this sense. Real political parties do in practice seem to be reluctant to bring into a government coalition parties who must be given cabinet portfolios, but whose votes are not essential to the survival of the government. Perhaps the best-known exposition of this basic argument can be found in another of the modern classics of political science, *The Theory of Political Coalitions*, by William Riker.

We saw when discussing how to play the game for a share of a fixed Trough that a large change in a party's seat total can have little or no effect on its bargaining power while, conversely, a small change in legislative strength might have a big effect on its power. Interestingly, there is no clear evidence that real political parties

113

exploit their bargaining advantage to the utmost in this regard, with very small parties getting as big a slice of the cake as very large ones when both are in an equally strong bargaining position. There seems to be what political scientists have termed a strong 'proportionality norm', with parties tending to get seats at cabinet in proportion to their legislative seat totals, although there is some bias in favour of smaller parties. This may well have to do with the chance that voters in subsequent elections may punish parties which throw their weight about in what might be seen by cissies as a 'disproportional' manner, a real-world possibility that the game does not capture.

Notwithstanding the lack of empirical evidence, however, the theoretical possibility of a small party holding much larger parties to ransom is something that clearly disturbs those who oppose the introduction of proportional electoral systems, since proportional systems often produce coalition governments. Of the many arguments against proportional representation and coalition government (most of them very bad) this is the most sophisticated. The point is basically that, instead of seriously underrepresenting small parties, which is what happens under a 'first-past-the-post' electoral lottery, proportional representation systems seriously *overrepresent* them. This is not because proportional representation gives small parties more seats than they deserve, which almost never happens to any significant extent, but because giving a small party even its fair share of seats can sometimes allow it to wield a disproportionate amount of the bargaining power when it comes to forming a government. Whether they agree with this argument or not, playing Coalitions should give the players some insight into it.

If government parties are only interested in sharing out the contents of a Trough and nothing else, then, while carrying no passengers, they should none the less comprise a set of parties that between them have a majority of seats in the legislature. 'Minority' governments which do not control a majority of seats should never form. A minority government, after all, faces a majority opposition that has enough votes to win the prize and a clear incentive to do so. Something must clearly be wrong if a majority opposition does not claim the prize in such a case. We shouldn't find minority coalitions winning the prize in the basic game, and we don't find many minority governments in some real-world political systems. But minority governments are really quite common in other political systems suggesting that, notwithstanding the cynics, real politicians may be interested in something more than merely sticking their noses in the Trough. That 'something' is most likely policy, and policy pay-offs are what characterize most of the game's variations.

Having allocated cabinet positions, therefore, the other important matter that real coalition partners must settle before they can form a working coalition government is an agreed government policy on the important issues of the day. Both in the game and in reality, the need to agree a government policy means that coalitions involving parties with similar policies will be preferred to coalitions involving parties with policies that are wildly different. Thus a party's ability to get into government, both in the game and in reality, is affected not only by its size but also by its policies. Large parties with extreme policy positions may well be able to extract much less out of the system than small parties with central policy positions that make them more attractive coalition partners.

The combined effects of party strength and party policy illustrate some of the fascinating intricacies of coalition bargaining in the real world. The complex interaction between size and bargaining power, for example, becomes even more intriguing when party policy is also considered. Since parties with policy positions that are closer to the centre of the policy spectrum will appeal to more potential coalition partners, we have just seen that it follows small parties near the centre of the spectrum will be better placed to get into government than small parties at the extremes. The one-dimensional version of the game illustrates the potential power of small centre parties very clearly indeed. A small party at the median position, in the sense that it can form a majority equally well with parties to its right as it can with parties to its left, can be in a very powerful position indeed, being very difficult to keep out of government. A small party at the end of the policy scale, in contrast, can be utterly out of the frame when it comes to coalition bargaining.

Once more, the game allows people to get a feel for this particular argument about the real world. You should never forget, of course, that the small party at the centre of the spectrum will have a policy position that will never be too far from the preferred position of most voters. In this sense the 'sophisticated' argument against proportional electoral systems that we discussed in the previous section misses an important point. The superior bargaining power of a small central party is exercised in favour of a policy position favoured by more voters than any other, a use of power that might well be seen for this reason as being an entirely appropriate feature of coalition bargaining.

If the coalition game is played using party positions on more than one dimension of policy, then there may well be no 'central' party in a position to dominate the business of coalition bargaining. If the coalition simply has to negotiate a policy position on two dimensions then, as we saw when discussing how to play the game, bargaining is likely to be chaotic and unstable. In the real world, for the most part, coalition bargaining does not tend to be as unstable as this, suggesting that something else is going on. That something else might possibly be a factor that is captured in those versions of the game which involve setting coalition policy by giving the power to do this to a party that controls the relevant cabinet portfolio. If you play these variations of the game, then you may well find that there are indeed stable outcomes of coalition bargaining. One implication of this is that it may in the real world be the division of labour in policy-making between different cabinet ministers in charge of different departments with responsibility for making and implementing policy in different areas, that gives some sort of structure to the business of setting policy in a coalition cabinet. A general introduction to the politics of government coalitions, which deals in simple terms with the role of party policy in all of this, can be found in Michael Laver and Norman Schofield's *Multiparty Government*. Once more, *Private Desires, Political Action* provides a general discussion of the main themes and points to further reading.

Whatever else the game might show, it highlights the characteristic mixture of conflict and co-operation that runs through real coalition bargaining. Parties want to get into government, either to stick their noses into the Trough or to implement particular policies. Before they can do this they must make compromises in the knowledge that the compromises they make could turn out to harm them. In certain circumstances, indeed, the necessary compromises may seem so potentially dangerous that the party gives up all hope of getting into office in a particular session, contents itself with opposition, and bides its time until the next election.

REAL COALECTIONS

Real-life politics is not just about elections, not just about coalition formation, not just about both of these things, but also about the complex interaction between the two. (You will be delighted to hear that political scientists are only just beginning to get to grips with this interaction so that there is, as yet, nothing to read on the matter that is both interesting and accessible.) Members of coalition governments, for example, have to keep several of their many eyes fixed firmly on the next election. Parties fighting a 'robust' election campaign and inflicting damage all around them, by the same token, would be foolish to forget about the coalition negotiations that will inevitably follow this, when deals will need to be done with electoral opponents.

One of the ways in which the politics of coalition have an impact on the next election is that parties tend to get lumbered in the public mind with the policies of a coalition to which they just belonged. Indeed the final straw that breaks a particular coalition's back is often some relatively minor crisis that confronts one of the members with being associated in government by some policy position that it knows offers a strong possibility of subsequent electoral disaster.

Similarly, if parties know that no single one of them will win an overall majority in an election, and this is of course the normal situation in most parliamentary democracies, then they simply cannot ignore the business of coalition bargaining when they set about fighting an election campaign. Indeed, a very fundamental question that each party must ask itself in such circumstances is whether or not its strategic objective is to maximize votes, or to get into the coalition that will subsequently form, given the distinct possibility that these two motivations may pull party strategy in opposite directions.

Finding the best all-round strategy in these circumstances is a complex business, particularly because the ways in which voters might use elections to punish parties for their performance in office are not very well understood. Politicians who go into government clearly do keep an eye on the next election, at which they will be called to account, and this clearly does stop them from deviating too dramatically from their established electoral policy positions. This has the clear implication that some policy concessions in office may simply be too big, measuring the costs of these in terms of subsequent electoral losses. Ultimately, this electoral discipline is one of the things that provides incentives for parties to look for coalition partners with similar, rather than different, published policies, even if intrinsically the parties themselves do not care very much about policy. In this sense, a party's electoral policy position is part of its stock-in-trade, a real political asset that it may well be unwilling to compromise for short-term political gain.

The electorate may also punish parties at elections for reasons that are not covered by the game or its variations—though some of these could be incorporated by truly determined players. There is, for example, a popular belief, at least among some politicians, that voters will punish those parties that they hold responsible for bringing down a government, thereby forcing them out to the polling booths on a wet and windy evening. There can thus be quite a bit of manœuvring when a government is about to fall, in an attempt to pin the blame for the collapse on one party or another. As we have seen, one of the reasons why parties may not exploit their bargaining advantage to the maximum when looking for a share of cabinet seats is that they may fear that voters will punish them for being too 'greedy' if they look for more cabinet positions than they are entitled to by virtue of their share of legislative seats. Thus parties can be punished, or at least politicians may be afraid that they will be punished, for being too tough with coalition partners, as well as for being too soft and going along with a coalition policy that differs wildly from party policy.

A SOPHISTICATED GAME

9 Agenda

A game for five or more experienced players/crews, who should have tried at least a couple of the previous games before they turn their hands to Agenda. The game should take about an hour and a half.

The players/crews are members of a committee and each has strong feelings on a number of matters. Success or failure depends to a large extent on the ability of players to get their way by manipulating the rules of committee procedure. There is an incentive to come to arrangements with others, but there is also the possibility of going it alone and simply outwitting them.

EQUIPMENT AND CREWS

A bundle of money and a Trough; a pack of playing-cards; a blackboard or large sheet of paper; a timer; a gavel or other hammer; the proverbial brown envelopes; badges or costumes to distinguish crews. Players/crews choose names from the following list:

- The Mothers of Invention
- The Velvet Underground
- Country Joe and the Fish
- The Psychedelic Furs
- The Sex Pistols
- Blondie
- NWA

RULES

1. Each round of play represents one meeting of a committee. The players are committee members and start the game with

100,000 each in walking-around money. At the start of each meeting, a committee Chair must be selected. The first Chair is the eldest player or crew Boss, and players subsequently take turns to chair committee meetings in order of age. The Game Overall Director (GOD) knows the ages of all players, and her decision is final in the event of a dispute. Alternatively some alternative criterion, such as beauty or intelligence, might be chosen by mutual agreement among the players and applied in a very subjective manner by GOD.

2. Each meeting will decide upon how the committee's budget will be allocated between four important spending areas. Committee members have to pay to play, each throwing 40,000 into the Trough at close range before the meeting begins.

3. Committee members, including the Chair, have preferences about how the budget should be allocated. In order to discover these preferences, the pack of cards is shuffled meticulously by GOD and dealt face down, a card at a time, to each player in turn until the pack is exhausted. Some players will have one more card than others but that, of course, is life. Each suit represents a particular spending area:

- clubs represent defence;
- spades represent public works;
- hearts represent social welfare;
- diamonds represent industry.

The players find out how they feel about the world by adding up the face value of the cards they hold in each suit (court cards, representing the aristocracy, naturally count for nothing). The total face value of cards a player holds in a particular suit represents the player's preferred level of spending, in thousands, on the policy area in question. Thus a face value of twelve in hearts means that you would like to see 12,000 spent on social welfare, while a face value of six in spades means that you would like 6,000 spent on public works. Players may, if they wish, show all or part of their hands to others, although they would be mad to do so.[3]

---

[3] As was the case with Free Riding, Nature may save time by allocating each crew an arbitrary set of preferences in a slip of paper before the game starts. This saves time and the need to deal and count cards. Once more, the advantages of speed must be weighed against the potential for paranoid players to feel that they are being manipulated by Nature.

4. After the cards have been dealt, the committee members have three minutes, timed to the second by GOD, to make a proposal on each spending area. They do this by writing each of their four proposals *legibly* on a separate piece of paper and handing it to the Chair. Each proposal must contain the name of the proposer, the issue to be discussed, and a proposed level of expenditure. Committee members are free, if they choose to do so, not to make a proposal on some spending area or, indeed, not to make any proposal at all. The Chair is not allowed to make any proposal and by way of compensation is allowed to talk to GOD while mere committee members ponder their proposals. If mere committee members talk to GOD at any stage during the game, they are sent to the nearest psychiatric hospital or punished in some other way that seems appropriate at the time to GOD.

5. Before each committee meeting can start, the Chair has three minutes to produce an agenda. This is a list of various proposals for spending in different areas that will be discussed by the committee, giving an order in which these will be discussed. Mere committee members are allowed to let their hair down and talk to *each other* while the Chair is about this important work or to repair to the nearest bar or motel room.

6. The agenda must include at least two proposals on each spending area, unless less than two proposals have been made on a particular area. If only one or two proposals have been made for a particular area, then these *must* be put on the agenda. If no proposal has been made in an area, then none will appear. If more than two proposals have been made in some spending area, then the Chair may choose which to include. The order in which proposals are placed on the agenda is entirely at the discretion of the Chair.

7. At the end of the three-minute agenda-construction period, the Chair must write the agenda *legibly* on the blackboard or large sheet of paper. This agenda must include the proposals chosen and the order in which these are to be discussed. Beside each proposal should be written the name of the proposer, the spending area concerned, and level of expenditure involved. Once the agenda is on the board, the Chair must then bang the table vigorously with the gavel or hammer to call the committee members to order. *All* types of private interaction between the players, even the meeting of

eyes over (or the rubbing of legs under) a crowded committee table, must stop at once.

8. Once the committee is in session, all remarks must be addressed to the Chair. Any committee members holding a private conversation with each other must stop if called to order by the Chair. Once a player has been called to order in this way, any further disobedience of this rule may result in the offender being expelled ignominiously from the meeting.

9. Polite language must be used at all times while the committee is in session. If one committee member wishes to insult another committee member or the Chair, the insult must be prefaced with the words, 'with respect' (for a mild insult), 'with the greatest respect' (for a moderately hurtful insult), and 'with the greatest possible respect' (for a perfectly vile insult). Any player using each type of insult more than once during a committee meeting, or not prefacing an insult with the appropriate incantation, may be deemed to be out of order by the Chair and expelled from the meeting.

10. Expelled committee members may not vote again in that session, although they continue to receive any pay-offs due to them. They may converse with other players only during a recess (see below). Any committee member talking to someone who has been expelled may also be expelled from the meeting.

11. The proposals are discussed in the order in which they appear on the agenda, unless this order is changed by a procedural motion (see below). When a proposal comes up for discussion, the Chair reads it out and asks if there is a seconder. If there is no seconder, the other committee members must do their utmost not to laugh, the proposal fails, and discussion moves to the next item on the agenda. If there is a seconder, then the proposal becomes a substantive motion before the committee. No other substantive motion may be discussed until the fate of the current substantive motion has been decided.

12. Once a motion has been proposed and seconded, the Chair asks for discussion. If there is no discussion, then the motion is put immediately to the vote. If discussion is requested by any committee member, then the Chair must allow one speech for, and one speech against, the motion. At any stage in the discussion after this, the Chair may decide to put the motion to the vote, unless

there is an outstanding amendment or procedural motion (see below).

13. The Chair may not vote on any motion, except in the event of a tie, in which case the Chair has a casting vote.

14. Once a substantive motion on a particular spending area has been carried, no further discussion may take place in that meeting of the committee on the spending area in question. The motion that has been carried becomes the policy of the committee for that session. The Chair writes this decision on the board and removes any further proposals on this issue from the agenda.

15. Once a substantive motion has been carried or defeated, discussion moves on to the next proposal on the agenda and proceeds according to rules 8–13. Additional proposals concerning spending areas for which policies have not yet been decided by the committee may then be discussed.

16. *Procedural motions*. The following procedural motions may be proposed by any committee member except the Chair at any stage. Once a procedural motion has been proposed and seconded, it may be discussed before being put to the vote. Voting on procedural motions takes precedence over voting over any other motion or amendment. Procedural motions may not be amended. No more than one procedural motion may be under discussion at any one time. The procedural motions that may be put are:

A recess

If a proposal for a recess is carried, then the committee goes into a three-minute recess, timed by the Chair. During this recess, committee members may hold private conversations among themselves. This is the only way that committee members may legally communicate with one another while committee is in session. Players may also converse during a recess with members of the committee who have been ejected for various transgressions, and may trade insults freely and without qualification. While all of this is going on, the Chair may talk to, and even seek advice from, GOD. At the end of the recess, signalled by loud banging of the gavel or hammer by the Chair, all private conversations must stop immediately and all further remarks must be addressed through the Chair.

Agenda

An agenda motion

Before any particular item on the agenda is discussed, a player may propose that an item further down the agenda be discussed first. If such a proposal is carried, then the specified motion is discussed as if it were the next item on the agenda. Alternatively, a player may propose that voting on a particular motion be deferred until a specified point on the agenda has been reached. If such a proposal is carried, then discussion moves on to the next item on the agenda.

Next business

At any time during the discussion of a particular substantive motion, a player may propose 'next business'. If this proposal is seconded and carried, then discussion of the current item on the agenda is immediately terminated. Discussion moves on to the next item on the agenda and a vote is never taken on the item which was terminated.

No confidence in the Chair

If a motion of no confidence in the Chair is seconded and carried, then the player in the Chair must immediately stand down in favour of the proposer of this motion. If the no-confidence motion is carried, then all players, except the new Chair, must pay GOD a forfeit of 20,000. If the no-confidence motion is defeated, then the proposer must pay the victorious Chair 20,000.

17. All votes are carried if more committee members vote for than against and defeated if more vote against than for. All voting is by show of hands. The player in the Chair may not vote on any matter, except to break a tie. Any committee member may abstain on any vote.

18. Play continues until the agenda is exhausted. This will happen either when every proposal on it has been voted upon, or when a policy has been agreed on each of the four spending areas, since all remaining proposals will have been deleted. If no decision has been reached at this stage on one or more of the four issues, then the expenditure on this policy area for this session is set at zero and pay-offs are made accordingly.

19. *Pay-offs.* Once the agenda has been completed as described in rule 18, the committee meeting is over and the members are

paid off. Each player, including the Chair, gives their hand of cards to GOD who notes down their preferences. Each player is paid on the basis of how close each committee decision is to her own preferred policy, as revealed in her hand of cards. If the total expenditure decided by the committee on a particular issue is identical to a committee member's preferred expenditure, then the person in question receives 20,000 from GOD. For every 1,000 that the committee decision differs from the player's preference, 1,000 is deducted from this 20,000 pay-off. If the committee member's preference on some spending area differs from the committee decision by more than 20,000, then all of the other players do their best to keep a straight face, while the person concerned receives *no pay-off whatsoever for any spending area decided by the committee.* These pay-offs are made for each of the four spending areas, bearing in mind that, if no committee decision is reached in relation to some area, then its expenditure on that area is zero.

20. Once the cards have been handed in at the end of each session of the committee, a new session is convened, Chaired by the next youngest (or most beautiful or intelligent) player and play continues as at rule 2. GOD works out the pay-offs for the previous round and distributes these in brown envelopes during the new round of play.

21. The game ends when every player has had a chance to be Chair, or when the time-limit expires. The player with the most money is, of course, the loser. Players compete vigorously with each other to lose this game, which is designed as a complete antidote to more conventional games in which winning is the only thing.

VARIATIONS

Amendments

At any stage during the discussion of a substantive motion, any committee member may propose an amendment to it. This amendment must make a proposal on the same issue as the substantive motion but may alter the proposed level of expenditure by up to three thousand. If an amendment is proposed, then the Chair must ask for a seconder. If there is no seconder, then the amendment fails and discussion continues on the substantive motion. If there is a seconder, then the Chair must ask for discussion of the amendment. One speech for and against the amendment must be allowed, after which it must be put to the vote. The amendment is carried if more committee members vote for it than against it, in which case the amended motion becomes the new substantive motion. If the amendment is defeated, then discussion and voting continue on the original substantive motion. No more than two amendments are allowed on any single substantive motion. Passing an amendment to a substantive motion, of course, does not mean that the motion proper has been passed. This must still be put to a vote and can still be defeated.

Qualified majority voting

The number of votes in favour needed to pass a substantive motion (though not a procedural motion) is set above the simple majority threshold, at three-quarters of the number of committee members. Thus in a five-person committee, the number of voters in favour would need to be four; in a six-person committee it would need to be five; in a seven- or eight-person committee it would need to be six; and so on.

Compound proposals

Up to four proposals may be made by each committee member; each proposal *must* refer to more than one spending area.

Rolling logs

This variation is almost, but not quite, a whole new game and can be played with or without qualified majority voting. If five or six players are involved, then the jacks are taken out of the pack, otherwise the full pack is used. The deal to determine how committee members feel about the world takes place as at rule 3. This time court cards represent the aristocracy, and are obviously the only cards worth a damn in the game. The game proceeds as in the basic game, with the following differences:

- Committee members do not make proposals for agenda items, so rule 4 does not apply. The Chair must instead construct an eight-item agenda of simple proposals, each of which comprises a proposal to spend 20,000 on one of the four spending areas.

There must be two proposals for each of the four spending areas.

• Committee members only get a pay-off for spending areas in which they hold court cards—they do not get paid at all for spending in other areas. If a proposal is passed, all players holding court cards in that area get 20,000, all other players get nothing.

HOW TO WIN AGENDA

Playing this game demands very different skills, depending upon whether you are the committee Chair or a mere committee member.

The Chair

Just because the Chair of the committee can neither vote nor propose motions, never think that this player is at the mercy of mere committee members. Far from it. It should quickly become clear as you play the game that the ability of the Chair to set the committee's agenda is a very important source of power.

In the basic game, when each proposal before the committee deals with a single area of spending, the ideal policy position of the median committee member should prevail over any other proposal if this policy is put to a simple majority vote, for reasons that were explored when we discussed Coalitions. If the Chair has a preferred level of spending that is closer to the level proposed by the median committee member than to any other proposal, then the median voter's proposal should be included on the agenda and the Chair can let matters take their course. If, however, the Chair has an ideal policy position that differs radically from those of the median committee member, then she has considerable scope for manipulation of the eventual outcome.

Imagine for example that the Chair prefers a level of spending that is much higher than the median. The Chair could include the proposal closest to her ideal position, as well as another proposal to spend even more money than this (if one is available). A majority of committee members, presented with these alternatives, can do no better than to vote for the proposal most preferred by the Chair, assuming that a majority prefers this to the possibility of spending nothing at all on the area in question. They would prefer the proposal made by the median committee member if they should somehow get this, but it is not being offered to them by the Chair.

We might think of this as rather obvious manipulation by the Chair—achieved by putting on the agenda only proposals that she herself prefers to alternatives that are preferred by a majority of the committee. There may well, however, be sneakier ways to achieve the same thing. Imagine that you, as Chair, prefer quite low levels of spending, sufficiently low that you would rather spend nothing at all than go along with the spending plans of the median committee member. If two very high proposals were made, then you could include these and no others, in the expectation that a majority of committee members would vote against both, preferring to see spending set at zero rather than at these high levels. Or you could include one very high proposal and one much closer to your own heart. The possibilities, as I'm sure you can see, are enormous, though they depend upon the precise distribution of preferences in each case, and the precise proposals that committee members opt to make.

Of course, cute committee members will suspect that something is going on and will try and outsmart you (a matter to which we will shortly return) so it won't all be plain sailing. You will none the less have the great advantage in all of this that no committee member will know your preferences on any issue, while you will not be forced to give anything away by having to make proposals in public, so that committee members won't have all of the information that they need if they are to outsmart you with any regularity.

Once the game moves to the variations, the role of the Chair will change too. The qualified majority voting rule opens up the possibility that no proposal, even the ideal policy position of the median voter, can win a majority vote and greatly enhances your ability to manipulate things as Chair. Perhaps, for example, committee members controlling more than 30 per cent of the votes (two out of a committee of five, say) prefer a much lower level of spending than the one proposed by the median committee member. If you share this view as Chair, you can let the median committee member's proposal go to a vote, confident that the power of the blocking minority will be used in your interest. Even if people know your preferences, it will be hard to accuse you of manipulation. They may suspect that your 'naïve' strategy of putting the 'most popular' proposal to the meeting, only to see it defeated, is far from naïve at all, but you can just smile sweetly and it will be harder than hell for them to prove anything. Qualified majorities are a cute chairperson's dream!

The same thing can be said about compound proposals. If more than one spending area is up for discussion in a series of proposals, then things start to get really wild. There's now at least a chance that no single proposal can win majority support against all others, for reasons discussed above when we looked at the two-dimensional version of Coalitions. This is an environment that is more or less the Garden of Eden for a wily Chair, who can usually figure out a selection of proposals, and a sequence in which to put them, that will guarantee a result quite close to her ideal policy.

At the risk of making things look more complicated than they are (and they *are* complicated) consider the situation in Table 9.1 showing a game with three committee members making compound proposals on defence and social welfare. Player A's preference is for defence and social welfare spending both to be set at 10,000. Player B prefers defence spending at 20,000 and welfare spending at 10,000. Player C prefers defence spending at 15,000 and social welfare spending at 17,000. There are three proposals I, II, and III to be dealt with, allocating spending as shown in the three rows of the table labelled I, II, and III respectively. Note that in a majority vote Proposal I beats Proposal II (Players A and B both prefer I to II), Proposal II beats Proposal III (Players A and C both prefer II to III), but Proposal III beats Proposal I (Player B and C both prefer III to I). This example shows a 'voting cycle' at work. If the players could make and remake these proposals at will and

Table 9.1

Proposed spending on ('000s):			Pay-off to Player (preferred spending level, '000s)		
	Defence	Welfare	A(10, 10)	B(20, 10)	C(15, 17)
I	12	10	38	32	30
II	13	15	32	28	36
III	18	12	30	36	32
0	zero	zero	20	10	8

continue until one proposal beats all others, then they would be sitting at the committee table until one of them died of exhaustion, since no one of these proposals can beat both of the other two in a majority vote.

However, players can't make and remake proposals at will. Instead, they can consider only proposals that have been offered to them by the Chair, and must consider these in a particular order. Note that the Chair has an additional implicit proposal to play with, a *status quo* in which nothing is spent on either policy area if the committee members cannot agree, with pay-offs to the players as listed in Table 9.1 in the row labelled 0. Now hold on to your hats and see what opportunities this type of situation, which will be endemic when several issues are considered at the same time, offers a smart Chair.

The first thing the Chair has to do is to decide how 'sophisticated' the players are, in the sense of being able to see beyond the ends of their noses to the eventual consequences of their actions, rather than simply voting naïvely on each proposal as it comes up, in accordance with their preferences and without regard for the effects of such votes. There are six agendas that the Chair can set using these three proposals, simply reflecting the six ways that three proposals can be ordered. These are set out in Fig. 9.1. (If you know all about this type of analysis already, then you won't find this figure complex. If you don't already know about the huge potential power of an agenda, then I make no apologies for the complexity of the figure and suggest that you should really make an effort to master what is going on. This is complicated stuff, but it is something you'll be able to put to good effect over and over again in your future dealings with the rest of the world.)

Imagine first that the other players are totally naïve, simply voting at each point on the agenda for the alternative that they prefer. Since all three players prefer all three proposals to the *status quo* of spending nothing, the first proposal on the agenda, which pits some proposal against spending nothing, will win. Playing against dunderheads such as this, the Chair simply puts the alternative she most likes at the head of the agenda and the players will respond by thinking 'Sonofagun—that's *much* better than nothing; I'll vote for it.' They fail to notice that there are proposals that they like much better lower down the agenda, which will now not get

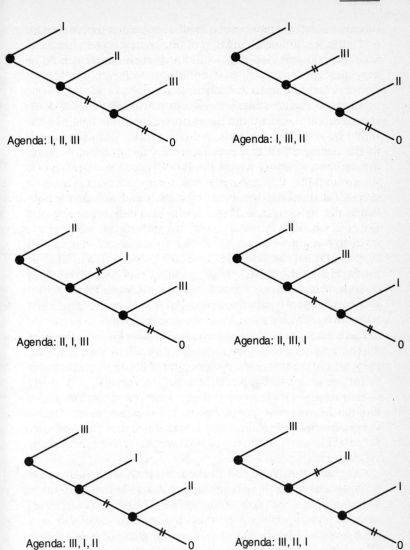

Agenda: I, II, III

Agenda: I, III, II

Agenda: II, I, III

Agenda: II, III, I

Agenda: III, I, II

Agenda: III, II, I

Fig. 9.1 The six different agendas for three proposals, I, II, and III

discussed. They thereby point a loaded shotgun at their right foot and enthusiastically pull the trigger, just because it looks like a real nice thing to pull. You might think that such morons would be easy meat for even a half-way sophisticated Chair, but hold your horses before coming to *that* conclusion.

Smarter committee members, of course, will cast their eye down the agenda and vote on the current proposal in the light of what might be available later. Look at Agenda (I, II, III) in the top left of the figure, which first puts Proposal I to the meeting. Semi-dunderheads who prefer Proposals II or III might vote against I on the grounds that this disposes of one alternative, leaving the field clear for a shoot-out between Proposals II and III that are both listed later on the agenda. Player B, who likes Proposal III best, and Player C, who likes Proposal II best, might think this way, but one of them has got to be wrong! If they go ahead and vote against Proposal I, then the field is left open for Proposals II and III to be pitted against the *status quo* of spending nothing. Given these options, Player C likes Proposal II best of all, while Player A likes Proposal II best of what's left. Proposal II is next on the agenda and wins the vote, with Players A and C voting in favour.

This means, of course, that Player B, who likes Proposal II least of all the proposals, was not so smart after all in voting against Proposal I in the first place. A sophisticated Player B would be able to foresee what will happen if Proposal I is defeated, and so will vote strategically for Proposal I when it arises, *even though she prefers Proposal III, and even though Proposal III does appear later on the agenda*. In effect, she realizes that Proposal III cannot succeed once Proposal I has been eliminated and Player A, for this reason, shifts allegiance to Proposal I.

Mercifully, this is the end of the line—if all of the players are sophisticated, then there is nothing that any of them can do to improve on this outcome for themselves. The bottom line is that, since all players prefer any proposal to the *status quo* in this case, once Proposal I has been put first on the agenda, to defeat it in effect means pitting Proposal II against Proposal III, a vote that Proposal II will win. Those who prefer Proposal I to Proposal II (Players A and B in this case), will thus vote for Proposal I as soon as this is put, to avoid that shoot-out between Proposals II and III, the results of which they can foresee.

This may seem hard stuff to get on top of, but diagrams like those in Fig. 9.1 show you how to think through the strategic impact of an agenda in a more systematic manner. Take the top-left agenda (I, II, III). The branching diagram shows that, first, Proposal I is put to the committee. If this wins, then it is put into effect; if it loses, then Proposal II is put. If this wins, it is put into effect; if it loses, then Proposal III is put. If it wins, it is put into effect; if it loses, then the *status quo* prevails. Smart players will work back from the end of the agenda. They will see that if they get down to the last item, and the choice is between Proposal III and the *status quo*, then all three players will certainly vote for Proposal III. There can be no doubt about that.

In other words, the *status quo* is not, in a strategic sense, ever going to prevail. It can thus be eliminated from strategic consideration, and the path to it in the diagram is blocked with two short parallel lines. This means, when you think about it, that if you get to the middle item on the agenda when Proposal II is being discussed, that the certain choice is between Proposal II and Proposal III. Given this certain choice, Proposal II will defeat Proposal III. Thus Proposal III, like the *status quo*, is never going to prevail, given this agenda. Thus the path to it is also blocked with two parallel lines, since it is a strategic distraction to consider it further. And *this* means that when you are at the first item on this agenda, that the real choice it between Proposal I and Proposal II. In effect, this particular agenda poses a straightforward *de facto* strategic choice to sophisticated players. Proposal I beats Proposal II in this event. In other words, with sophisticated players, *the choice of this particular agenda amounts to the choice of Proposal I as the eventual outcome*.

The other possible agendas are each analysed in the same way in Fig. 9.1. The top two agendas put Proposal I first and lead to the selection of Proposal I. The middle two agendas put Proposal II first and lead to the selection of Proposal II. The bottom two agendas put Proposal III first and lead to the selection of Proposal III. Leaving aside the possibility for players to influence the agenda by making amendments, if these are allowed, or procedural motions (both vital matters to which I will return when discussing strategies for committee members, below), the Chair, by being able to choose the agenda is in effect able to choose the outcome.

It is impossible to overemphasize this power, which is exercised without the Chair ever casting a single vote or uttering a single word of persuasion. The Chair in effect sets up the structure of decision-making to generate the outcome she wants. The only way she can come unstuck is by being wrong about the preferences of the players or their level of sophistication. The Chair will have to make guesses about these, a matter which obviously gives players an incentive to keep their cards very close to their chests. But players will have to reveal something about their preferences when they make proposals, and this will be the raw material that the Chair has to work with. (This is why players may, however, make proposals designed to conceal rather than reveal their preferences, another matter to which we will shortly return.)

Of course it is not always possible for the Chair to prevail over a committee by just using agenda power. If, for example, almost all members of the committee have at the top of their list some proposal that the Chair has at the bottom of her own list, then the Chair may be powerless to do anything about this, although even then this is not certain. In general, however, there are many, many situations in which the agenda power of the Chair is absolutely central to the final outcome of a committee's decision-making.

This has been exhausting stuff, I know, and we can finish our discussion of the Chair with a more relaxed consideration of some rather more rough-and-ready tactics that might be tried. Remember that the only way of getting rid of the Chair is with a costly vote of no-confidence. This gives the Chair a lot of latitude in interpreting the rules of procedure to her own advantage, in effect daring the committee members to try to unseat her. The Chair can pick and choose speakers, and will have discretion on what procedural motions to accept when several of these are proposed at the same time, as can often happen. The rules, dare I say it, can even be bent by the Chair. Committee members may grumble, but they will have to be pretty mad to risk a confidence vote unless they are both sure of success and confident that the new Chair will be better for them. Pushing committee members to the limits of this tolerance is just another of the ways in which the Chair can attempt to exploit her very privileged position.

The committee members
Having read all of this, you may be wondering whether there is

anything left to do for a mere member of the committee, other than be manipulated by the Chair. But have no fear, there is still plenty of action available. The two key sets of choices you have to make as a mere committee member, assuming that you do indeed vote in a sophisticated way along the lines of the previous discussion rather than like a dunderhead, relate to the proposals that you can make and the procedural motions that you can attempt to exploit.

We've just seen that you face a dilemma when making proposals in that, if you always propose spending patterns that are close to your own heart, then it will be easy for the Chair, not to mention the other committee members, to take account of this. Indeed, if you think that you have preferences that are likely to be close enough to the eventual outcome—probably because you have middle-of-the-road preferences on most issues—you could opt for total inscrutability and make no proposal at all, revealing nothing about your hand.

Failing this, you must come to terms with the fact that *no* spending level will come into effect unless *some* committee member proposes it. Given the likelihood that other committee members will have preferences that differ from yours, the only way to get something that is quite close to what you want is to propose it yourself—otherwise it will not even be on the agenda. While you might be tempted to propose something that is not what you want as a smokescreen, hoping that it will be misinterpreted by the Chair and the other players, the danger is that your proposal may ultimately be adopted, leaving you feeling pretty sick when the payoffs are made. Proposing something really off the wall is almost the same as proposing nothing at all, of course, since people probably won't believe that you mean what you say. It does, however, offer scope for the Chair to include your proposal as part of some devious strategy of her own so you might do this if you think that your interests are really quite similar to those of the Chair.

In general, every time you make proposals, speak to motions, propose amendments and vote, you send out signals to the other players, signals that they will be trying to decode. As a general principle, only if the signals you send out are completely random will it be impossible for the other players to decode these, and playing the game in a random manner has many other disadvantages.

135

Once you behave in a non-random way, your behaviour is open to interpretation.

The most intriguing possibilities occur when there may be several conflicting interpretations for some signal that you send out by your words or actions. An example of this arises when you just *know* that you're going to be on the losing side of a vote that you would of course have preferred to win. In this case you might decide, since it makes no difference to the outcome, to vote with the winning side against your own preferred option, to make it more difficult for others to deduce your true preferences from your voting record. There is clearly a danger of things getting impossibly complicated, but remember that you do not really want the others to work out that you are trying to outsmart them. It may well be, therefore, that the simplest moves are the best, provided that you understand their consequences. If you seem to be playing a straightforward game, then your opponents may conclude that you are being simple-minded and are therefore easy to outsmart. A general rule of thumb in this game is to look for clever strategies that involve simple moves.

You have a whole range of additional tactics you can use as a 'mere' committee member. These arise from the possibility of proposing amendments to substantive motions, and from the range of procedural motions at your disposal.

We have already seen that the order in which proposals are discussed can have a huge effect on the outcome, to the extent that being in a position to dictate this order can sometimes be tantamount to being in a position to dictate the outcome. Several of the procedural motions open to you as a committee member provide methods for changing this order. Agenda motions move items up and down the agenda, while 'next business' scraps motions without a vote. The reasons why you might want to do either of these things should by now be relatively obvious. You may, for example, be in favour of moving to 'next business' rather than voting on some substantive proposal because you would rather conceal information about your preferences or your deviousness at some particular stage in the proceedings.

By far the most dramatic effects, however, can be achieved with agenda motions, for reasons that should be obvious from the discussion of the agenda power of the Chair. In the crude example set out in the figure above, choosing the agenda amounted to choosing the final outcome. Thus imagine that the Chair had announced that the agenda of proposals was (I, II, III) as set out in the top-left diagram in Fig. 9.1. When the committee is filled with sophisticated members, as we have seen, this results in Proposal I being approved as soon as it is put to the meeting. But what if the members themselves can vote on the agenda, as they can when they vote on agenda motions? A motion to take Proposal III first, for example, amounts to a proposal to change from the (I, II, III) agenda, to a (III, I, II) agenda shown in the bottom-left diagram in Fig. 9.1. This results in Proposal III being voted on first and carried. Players B and C both prefer Proposal III to Proposal I, so would be prepared to support this agenda motion. But then of course a second agenda motion that Proposal II now be taken first would create the (II, III, I) agenda that results in Proposal II being carried and is preferred to Proposal III by Players A and C. Thus this second agenda motion would also be carried. What has happened, of course, has been that, since details of procedure are determining the result, voting over the details of procedure has replaced voting on the substantive outcome as the location of the real strategic action.

All of this gives the players a great deal to think about, and might on the face of things appear to wrench power back from the Chair. However, the endless sequence of votes that was possible when the players could make proposals at will, that is usurped by a Chair who has the power to set an agenda, reappears if the players can make procedural motions at will. This is because procedural motions, as we have seen, become surrogates for substantive motions. In the midst of this potential chaos, key decisions on procedure are still taken by the Chair, decisions on which procedural motions to take, when to take them, which people to ignore when they clamour for attention, and so on. This dominant role in the procedural game will keep the whip hand firmly with the Chair, although it may at times offer intriguing possibilities for quick-witted committee members.

Amendments create a rather different set of strategic decisions for the players, but serve the same essential function of taking some level of control over the agenda back from the Chair and returning it to mere committee members. If amendments could simply propose anything, regardless of the substantive motion before the committee, then they would be just the same as a completely new proposal. But even the limited ability to propose an amendment varying the substantive proposal by no more than 3,000 offers some nice strategic options to the players. Most obviously, it allows the players to conceal some of their real feeling from the Chair at the point she is constructing the agenda, since there is always a subsequent option to vary the original proposal by 3,000, *in one direction or the other.*

The strategic possibilities of amendments go well beyond this, however. Going back to our ubiquitous example, if Player A's relative preference for proposals II and III were to be reversed, then proposal III would beat both I and II in a majority vote, and the Chair would need to use much more brutal measures in order to prevail. An amendment to change proposal III from 18,000 on defence and 12,000 on welfare to one of 17,000 on defence and 10,000 on welfare would have this effect. Player A now prefers III to II, and Proposal III can beat all comers. In this event, it will prevail among sophisticated players, regardless of the agenda. The real skill in this, of course, is in judging just the right amendment to switch some key voter, without giving away too much.

REAL AGENDAS

In many ways, the committee game is quite close to the way in which committees operate in the real world, so that a lot of what has already been said has actually been about real life. The main differences have to do with the complexity of the issues discussed, which are obviously much simplified when expressed as raw numbers in the game and offer many more possibilities in reality. The consequence of any complexity added in this way, however, is probably to exaggerate the main tendencies we have discussed above, and in particular the power of the Chair, rather than to negate them.

Even though committees are very, very common in the real world, the quite valid point of view that sitting in a committee is a very boring way to pass the day means that committees typically only get the respect they deserve from people who *really* know about politics at the sharp end. It may be something of an exaggeration to say that knowing how to work a committee is a skill that can make almost anyone more successful in this world, but it is not too wide of the mark. The big difference between committees and many of the other types of politics we have been talking about is that, in committees, what is going on is hand-to-hand combat. You can see the whites of your opponents' eyes, smell their fear and have a much better chance of being able to figure out what it is that they really want so as to build your own strategy around this valuable information. When you play the game in a real committee, you are playing with real people, not with pieces that move around a board. This is what makes committee games ideal for sophisticated players, who by definition make what they themselves do very carefully conditional on what they expect others to do, in the knowledge that those others are doing precisely the same thing. An excellent introduction to the strategic possibilities of agendas, together with pointers to further reading, can be found in Shepsle and Bonchek's *Analysing Politics*.

Probably the three key lessons about the real world to be learned from Agenda have to do with: first, the way you signal your preferences to sophisticated opponents by your own moves; second, the power that control over the agenda gives to a chair; third, the vital role of procedural matters. Next time you see a real committee player taking over the Chair and in the process giving up the chance to really speak her mind and vote of matters of burning concern to her, you'll know the chances of her getting what she wants have gone up, not down. Next time you see a group of experienced committee operators getting down and dirty over some 'trivial' matter of procedure, you can be almost certain that something *really* important is going on.

PUTTING THE POLITICS IN

10 Coalition Soccer

A fast-moving and invigorating game for 9–33 players of all ages; the number of players must be a multiple of three.

EQUIPMENT

A pack of playing-cards, a three-sided soccer pitch, a soccer ball, a whistle, a timer, and a referee who knows something about soccer. Corner flags and goals are a big help, but sports bags and coats can be used to mark these at a pinch.

THE BASIC GAME

1. The pitch

The pitch is an equilateral triangle, set out in one of two possible ways as shown in Fig. 10.1. There are no sidelines, only goal lines and a centre spot as marked. If nobody can be persuaded to mark out a triangular pitch in the proper manner, then tape, rope, traffic cones, spectators, or whatever comes to hand will just have to be laid out to mark the goal lines.

The size of the pitch depends to some extent on the number of players. For a five-a-side game, 75-metre (240-ft.) sides work well. Goal widths should be by prior agreement between the players. For the 75-metre pitch, 6-metre (18-ft.) goals work well.

As can be seen from Fig. 10.1, the difference between the two layouts is the relative positioning of goals and corner flags. The 'corner corners' layout places the goals closer to each other, leaves the goals more exposed for attacking play, but has more player congestion in the centre of the pitch. The 'corner goals' layout leaves the goals more protected from attack, but brings more of the pitch into routine play.

Corner corners

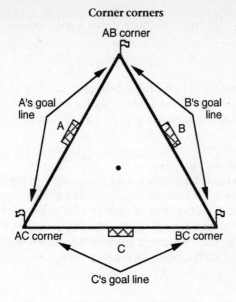

Corner goals

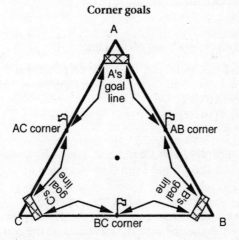

Fig. 10.1   Coalition Soccer pitches

2. Teams

In the basic game there are three teams, each with an equal number of players.

3. Kick-off

The team with the best-looking captain has first choice of goal; the ugliest captain has second choice of goal; the remaining captain takes the remaining goal, but gets to kick off from the centre spot.

4. Length of game

The length of each game is fixed by prior agreement between the players, though a reasonable choice is to have three thirteen-minute thirds. At the start of each third, the teams change goals anticlockwise, and the losing team kicks off. In the event of there being more than one losing team at the end of some third, the ugliest losing team captain kicks off.

5. Time-outs

Each team may call one time-out of three minutes during each third. Time-outs can only be called when the ball is out of play.

6. Ball-outs

When the ball crosses Team A's goal line:

- if Team B or C put it out, then Team A gets a goal kick;
- if Team A put it out on the AB side, then Team B gets a corner from the AB spot;
- if Team A puts it out on the AC side, then Team C gets a corner from the AC spot.

All goal and corner kicks are indirect. Equivalent rules are used if the ball crosses Team B's or Team C's goal line.

7. Scoring

When one team lets in a goal, *both other teams score a goal*. The winning team is the one with the most goals at the end of the third third. The sample scorecard shown in Fig. 10.2 may be some help in keeping track of this.

Team letting in goal			Score (Add one goal to the score of the other two teams)		
Blue	Green	Red	Blue	Green	Red

Fig. 10.2 Coalition Soccer scorecard

THE VARIATIONS

Circular pitch
The game is played on a circular pitch of, say, 40-metre radius. The three goals are placed equidistant from each other around the single circular goal line. Corner flags are placed on the goal line at the midpoints between each goal.

Moving goal posts
The game is played on the circular pitch. Teams are allowed, after a five-minute negotiating period before the game starts, to place their goals at any position on the circular goal line. Corner flags are placed on the goal line at the midpoints between each goal. The best-looking captain has first choice of goal position; the ugliest

captain has second choice of goal position; the remaining captain then places his or her team's goal, and furthermore gets to kick off from the centre spot. Before the end of each time-out, the team calling the time-out may reposition its goal. During the intervals between each third, any team may reposition its goal as it sees fit. Goals may not be moved while the ball is in play and the width of all goals must always remain the same as it was at the start of the game.

More teams

Playing on a circular pitch with either fixed or moving goals, the players may be divided into any number of teams that they might previously have agreed upon. As more teams are added, consideration should be given to increasing the radius of the pitch. Playing with eleven three-player teams and eleven goals, for example, a circular pitch with a radius of quite a bit more than 40 metres might well be advisable.

Changing sides

A fixed prize is agreed upon to be shared between the members of the winning team. All players contribute equally to this prize before the start of the game. Playing either the basic game or any of the above variations, players are allowed to change teams whenever the ball is out of play. A player who wants to change teams can leave his or her existing team without permission, but can only join a new team with the unanimous permission of its existing members. When changing teams, the player making the change must announce this clearly to all players in the game. There is no limit to the size of any team.

HOW TO WIN COALITION SOCCER

The first and by far the most important point to note about Coalition Soccer is that *it is possible to win without ever scoring a goal*, a feature that is a product of the game's unique scoring system and takes experienced soccer players some time to get the hang of. If two brilliant teams made up entirely of awesome soccer jocks slug it out without mercy, then every time they score a goal against each other they also score a goal for the third team, who may be complete nitwits on the soccer pitch but who will win the game none the less.

A second important point to note is that it is undoubtedly still a big advantage to be able to play soccer well, just as in the games that follow it will a big advantage to be able to play poker or darts.

Despite the need for real footballing ability, however, it is none the less quite difficult to win a game of Coalition Soccer without showing some serious political acumen. The reason for this is that it is just very hard, physically, for a team of, say, five players to hold out against a coalition of two teams fielding ten players between them. At the same time, other things being equal and just as in real-world soccer, the team that does best will be the team that can score the most goals. But it makes a big difference whom those goals have been scored against. Scoring them against the wrong team can lead to defeat rather than to victory.

The optimal strategy for the strongest team in terms of footballing skills, if it can get away with this, is to form an alliance with the weakest team and agree for them both to attack the second strongest team. Once the second strongest team has been satisfyingly hammered, the strongest team can then turn on its erstwhile coalition partner in the closing stages of the game and pull comfortably into the lead. We can thus imagine a game with the scorecard shown in Fig. 10.3.

The strongest team forges an alliance with the weakest team and between them they pound in eight goals against the hapless middle-ranking team, which doesn't stand a chance. As the end of the game approaches and the middle team is beaten and exhausted, the strong team suddenly rounds on its weak coalition partner and whacks in a couple of goals to give it a comfortable 10–2–8 victory.

Of course this is the ideal scenario for the strongest team—the other two teams are hardly going to sit around and let this happen to them without doing anything to counteract it. Anticipating the final defection of the strongest team, for example, the weakest team could break ranks much sooner and try to gang up with the middle team. After all, being a member of both of the game's coalitions should give the weakest team a very good chance of coming

Team letting in goal			Score (Add one goal to the score of the other two teams)		
Strong	Middle	Weak	Strong	Middle	Weak
	1		1		1
	1		2		2
	1		3		3
	1		4		4
	1		5		5
	1		6		6
	1		7		7
	1		8		8
		1	9	1	8
		1	0	2	8

Fig. 10.3 Sample Coalition Soccer game

out on top. And of course anticipating this particular possibility, the middle team might go to the strongest team earlier still, with some proposition or another.

What is clear is, first, that there is no strategy that clearly beats all others and, second, that being the weakest team at playing soccer need not be a huge disadvantage, particularly if this is compensated by an ability to make the best deals in the game.

The variations add spice to what will already have been quite a lively afternoon on the playing-field. The circular pitch may not change the game much in itself, but it does open up a range of other intriguing possibilities. To begin with, teams may give a physical manifestation to the coalitions that they form by moving their goal posts in some manner or another. One obvious possibility would be for teams in a coalition to place their goals side-by-side on the circle, facing their mutual enemy's goal. This would allow the coalition to deploy players more efficiently in defence of their goals, while freeing a decent number of players from defensive duties so that they can attack the enemy. It's not entirely clear that this is the best policy, however, since the combined coalition goals will provide an awfully big target for the opposition.

The strategic positioning of the goal posts will become particularly important, however, if the game is played by more than three teams. The scoring systems anyway force some quite complex strategic thinking once this happens, whatever the position of the goal posts. But obviously the positioning of ever more goals beside each other will create an ever-larger target, so that the trade-off between economies of scale in defence and the size of the target being offered to the enemy will become a real strategic issue.

Finally, the possibility that players may change teams in the middle of the game adds another layer of strategic interest. Since there is a fixed prize to be shared between players on the winning team, any team will want to win with as few players as possible. Yet at the same time, the more players in a team, the better the chance of actually being on the winning side. We might expect good players to attempt to negotiate a larger than average share of the winning team's pay-off in exchange for changing sides in the middle of the game. Certainly, the possibility for players to change sides will give an advantage to the team that is already in the lead. This is the team that is most likely to have a prize to share, and can use this prospect to attempt to seduce good players from rival teams if it feels the need to copper-fasten its position. The possibility for players to change sides also offers intriguing possibilities to a weak team that has done good deals, which might try to seduce a star player in the late stages of the game in an attempt to protect its gains against late coalition defections of the type that we have already discussed.

When a number of the variations are played at the same time, Coalition Soccer can become a pleasingly anarchic physical experience, rewarding real technical skill, while at the same time rewarding an ability to get on top of the politics of a situation. It is difficult to be more systematic about game-play than this, which is a very good reason to explore this type of interaction on the soccer pitch rather than by using some more boring analytical technique.

11 Coalition Poker

A card game for a maximum of seven players/crews. Each player gets three cards and must do deals with other players to build regular five-card poker hands, which rank as they do in the more usual version of poker.

EQUIPMENT

A pack of cards, a pile of money, some brown envelopes, a table, and some chairs. For the 'Banker' version, a large and dusty ledger is also needed.

CREWS AND TIME LIMITS

A time-limit must be agreed in advance and will be rigidly enforced by the Game Overall Director (GOD). If the game is played by crews, one member of each crew is designated as the crew Boss who makes the formal moves, although bargaining and negotiation are of course open to all. Crew names are chosen from the following list:

- Rockettes
- Cigarettes
- Suffragettes
- Space Kadettes
- Kos-Mik Rangers
- Perfect Strangers
- Sudden Dangers
- Rearrangers

VERSION 1: SHOWDOWN

1. The game has a succession of five-minute political nights, when loud music is playing and the lights are way down low, and

two-minute political days, when the lights burn brightly and there is nothing to be heard but the sound of silence. (See Chapter 1 for a discussion of day and night in politics.) At the start of each game, each player receives three cards from GOD, dealt from the bottom of a badly shuffled deck. Inexperienced or impatient players might agree to start each round with four cards each, so as to increase the probability of good hands.

2. Each player antes 10,000 at the beginning of each political night. The antes go into a Trough, the contents of which are shared out each day by the winning player(s). The ante may be scaled up or down by mutual agreement between the players before the game starts.

3. The nights are for wheeling and dealing and trading cards. Anything goes while GOD sleeps.

4. At the end of each night the music stops and there is a showdown. GOD takes a seat at the table as does each player. There is a hard seat for each player, and an especially comfortable seat for GOD. Two players who want to play a combined hand (see below) must sit next to each other and hold hands.

5. Starting with the player on her left-hand side and moving around the table clockwise, GOD asks each player in turn to play a hand.

6. A player plays a hand by putting one, two, or three cards face down on the table.

7. Two players sitting next to each other may play a combined hand, containing a maximum of five cards. The first player plays one, two, or three cards, the second plays one, two, or three cards. The players must also announce that they are playing a combined hand by putting a sealed brown envelope on the table between their cards, with a note inside specifying how the Trough is to be shared between them should their combined hand win.

8. The showdown takes place after the player sitting on the right hand of GOD has made her play. Any player sitting at the table too late to be asked by GOD to make a play cannot win the Trough. After GOD announces the showdown, all players turn their cards face up.

9. GOD gives the contents of the Trough to the player with the highest face-up hand. If this is a combined hand, GOD opens the sealed envelope and shares the contents of the Trough as specified

in the note inside. (For those unfamiliar with poker, the ordering of the hands is given in the Banker version, below.)

10. GOD deals a new card from the bottom of the pack to each player for each card that has been played, collects the cards that have been played, and half-heartedly shuffles these back into the pack. Night falls and play continues as at rule 2.

11. The winner is the player with the most money when the time-limit expires.

Betting variation

Instead of a simple showdown, as at rule 8 above, the players can bet before the showdown, as they do in many other types of poker game. In this case replace rule 8 as follows. The player on the left hand of GOD makes a bet by putting money in front of her on the table. The player on her left must either match this bet, raise it, or fold. Betting continues until all players have either folded or bet the same amount as each other. At this point, all money on the table is scooped up and put into the Trough by GOD. There is then a showdown during which any player who has not already folded may turn her cards face up, or may choose not to do so. Play continues as at rule 9.

VERSION 2: BANKER

1. The game lasts thirty minutes with no respite. The lights are turned way down low and *very* loud music pumps out of the sound system for the entire duration of the game. Dawn never breaks; the sound of silence is never heard. At the start of the game, each player receives three cards from GOD, dealt from the bottom of a frantically shuffled deck. Inexperienced or impatient players might agree to start each round with four cards each, so as to increase the probability of good hands.

2. GOD pretends to be a crazed philanthropic banker who pays single players, or pairs of players, for poker hands that they cash in at her bank. The value of the various hands is as follows (all straights and flushes are five-card hands):

One pair	1,000
Two pair	10,000

Threes	10,000
Straight	50,000
Flush	100,000
Full house	150,000
Fours	300,000
Straight flush	500,000
Royal flush	1,000,000

3. Any time a player or a pair of players feel like it, they can go to GOD and cash in a hand. GOD adds the pay-off to their bank account, which she keeps in a large and dusty ledger.

4. If a pair of players cash in a hand together, they must tell GOD how they want to share their worldly gains. GOD will, it goes without saying, respect their wishes.

5. GOD gives a new card from the bottom of the deck for every card cashed in, energetically shuffling back into the deck those cards that have just been cashed in.

6. When dawn does finally break after thirty minutes of mayhem, the player with the biggest bank account is the winner and is allowed to buy all of the other players a large round of drinks.

HOW TO WIN COALITION POKER

The Banker version

I'm going to start with the Banker version of Coalition Poker because in many ways its strategic logic is more straightforward. There are lots of books on how to win at poker, written by people who are much better poker players than I am. Fortunately, none of them has any relevance at all to Coalition Poker, except that they hammer home the relative probabilities of getting the various different poker hands from a fair deal in a range of different situations. No existing book, however, calculates the probability of putting together the various different poker hands, starting with three cards and combining these with one of a number of other players, each also holding three cards. No doubt these probabilities can indeed be calculated, but I have not calculated them, and do not have any inclination to do so. The pay-offs in the Banker version, therefore, are designed to reward those who combine with

151

others rather than to reflect real probabilities. Wizards at calculating these probabilities will quickly spot the good value hands on the menu and will in this way have some advantage over the other players. This is as it should be.

The Banker version of Coalition Poker is in fact a trading game, in which the only good hands are those that are put together as a result of forming coalitions with other players. It rewards people who can put together good deals by extracting as much as they can from a partner who has the other cards that make up a hand to be cashed in. There will be many head-to-head confrontations between people holding the two parts of a good hand, as each player will feel that it is *her* cards that make all the difference. How tough you can be in those head-to-heads will depend upon whether or not your cards give you any other options. If you do have other options, then you can walk away from a particular deal, and this will make you more powerful. This means that it will in practice be the person with the most *versatile* set of cards given the cards held by the other players, quite probably not the person with the best set of cards in their own right, who will be in the strongest position when it comes to doing deals.

Imagine, for example, that you hold three queens and are feeling pretty cool about this until you realize that three queens pay 10,000 while four queens pay 300,000. Getting together with the person who is holding on to that final queen adds 290,000 to the pay-off for that hand, and sharing out that 290,000 between you is going to involve some tough talking. Actually, depending on who holds what other cards, you may even be in the weaker position. If the deal breaks down you might find someone with a pair to make up a full house, but that's the best you can do. It's possible that the person holding that fourth queen also has a three and knows someone else with three threes. Even if they don't they might tell you that they do and, even if you find out that they're lying, you just can't get your hands on that 300,000 pay-off unless the person with the fourth queen will do a deal.

The bottom line, for any state of the game, is that every pair of players or crews has some best hand that they can put together between them, each with a specified pay-off. The player in the strongest intrinsic position at that stage will be the one participating in more valuable hands than any other. If the pace of the game is as hectic as it should be, however, the winner will be the person who can wheel and deal fastest and most effectively in this environment.

A big decision to make will be how much to reveal about your hand, since this information will be valuable to the other players. In the Banker version, however, it will almost always be necessary to be at least somewhat frank about your hand, since you will need to shop around between different deals, and in doing this will have to tell others what you've got in order to get anything out of them.

Something that many players fail to take into account is that this version of the game has a fixed thirty-minute free-form playing period, with no rounds. This means, unlike almost any other game, that the faster you do deals, the more money you make. It's no good spending ten minutes doing the very best deal in town if some other player has done ten deals at the same time as this, each for lesser amounts, but netting her much more cash overall. The game tends to reward instinctive deal-makers rather than those who are doggedly determined to squeeze the last drop of juice out of any given situation.

The Showdown version
The Showdown version of Coalition Poker is more intensely political than the Banker version, especially when the betting variation is played, as it should be at every opportunity. This is mainly because the strategic calculations about how much of your hand to reveal to the other players are far more complex in the Showdown version. Indeed the betting variation is essentially a full game of poker, with all of its magnificent richness, combined with the need to form coalitions in order to put together good hands.

When you play regular poker, almost the last thing in the world that you want is for other players to know precisely what you have in your hand before the showdown takes place. But in Coalition Poker you simply can't get a good hand without forming a coalition with others, and to do that you're going to have to show them what you've got. If the deal falls through, then they're going to *know* what you've got, and they can use this information against you. All of this makes for some pretty delicate interactions between players, of the 'I'll show you mine if you show me yours' variety.

In contrast to the Banker version, the highest hand in Showdown Coalition Poker wins the entire contents of the Trough, no matter how low that highest hand might be. This makes for some great, great bargaining possibilities. It creates situations in which good negotiators can do very well with what look like bad hands. And it creates huge incentives to break deals at the last minute.

Imagine, just to get a feel for working with a 'bad' hand, that there are three players, with hands as follows in mixed suits: (2, 3, 5), (2, 2, 3), (K, K, K). You've got the 235 hand, the lowest possible in regular poker. The KKK lady might try strutting around as if she owns the place but if you can find out what cards the others have, then things might not be so bad. If you find out about 223, for example, then you'll know that you can put together a full house with her, twos over threes. It's a winning hand against three kings and you can't put a better hand together using your cards and those of the other players, but is it the way for you to go?

Maybe not. Why not sidle up to the KKK lady and make her an offer, which she may take more as a threat. The offer will involve you in not going for a full house with 223, but rather in combining with KKK for—and this is the beautiful part of the deal—nothing better than the KKK she already holds! In effect you want a piece of her action for *not* doing a deal with the player holding 223!

If only life were that simple. In order to convince the KKK lady to go in with you, you'll have to mention something about 223 who, if she is not completely dumb, will also be trying to deal with KKK. And KKK plus 223 can make a 'kings over twos' full house if they get together. Actually, in this example you're all equal. Any deal between two of the three players, including you, will give them the strongest hand in the game, despite that sorry-looking 235 of yours. A lot will depend upon what has been revealed in the course of play about the content of the various hands. In practice, this will quite often be the case when the game is played between just three players and it is a good reason, if you do want things to get wild and woolly, to play with more than three.

Before we leave this particular three-player example, we can use it to see the incentives that might be there for players to break deals very late in the day. The KKK player has by far the strongest one-player hand in the game, and the highest hand wins all at the end of the day. If the KKK player sees no other deal has been done, then this gives her a *huge* incentive to renege on any deal *she* has done just seconds before any showdown. This would allow her to claim the whole prize single-handed. The other players know this, of course. Indeed it gives the other players a strong incentive not to put their faith in a deal with KKK, but rather to do a deal with each other. The clear possibility that KKK will renege late in the day and scoop the pool thus makes it hard for her to do deals with others. Strength can be weakness.

With six or seven players in on the action, the possibilities for putting together good hands will obviously increase a lot, and the likelihood that you will get to see every card in every player's hand will go down at the same time. You'll almost certainly only show your own hand to others on a 'need to know' basis. You *will* need to show parts of it if you are to entice other people into deals with you. But you should be able to arrange matters so that each player will be left wondering about at least some of the cards that you're holding. When it comes to the showdown, therefore, what turns up should not be a foregone conclusion.

The really big difference when the game is played with more than three players, of course, is the possibility of there being two or more coalitions. When only one coalition forms, then it is going to be pretty obvious who's going to win the showdown. This is not *certain*, of course, since the best a coalition might be able to manage might be two pairs, which would be beaten by a single player holding three of a kind who revealed nothing to anybody at any stage of the negotiations. When more players are involved and more than one coalition sets up in business for the showdown, however, things will be much less certain.

This also opens the way for bluffing by coalitions in the betting versions of the game, a possibility that will no doubt warm the cockles of any red-blooded poker player's heart and certainly brings Coalition Poker pretty much as close to real political life as it's possible for any card game to be.

12 Killer (Coalition Darts)

This is a darts game for between three and seven players/crews. Killer is played with relish by casual darts players in English pubs. As far as I can find out, and I may me wrong, it is almost never written about in dissertations on the game of darts.

EQUIPMENT

A dart board, some way of keeping the score, and three darts. Fussy players, of course, like to play with their own personal darts but this is strategically irrelevant. As for crew names, players should peruse earlier games, selecting those names with the most evocative darting resonances. If none such can be found, teams can be named in honour of former world darts champions.

RULES

1. All players begin the game as Punters. They must agree a time-limit for the game in advance, setting in motion a continuous soundtrack of loud and driving music that will end when the game is over.

2. Punters, beginning with the shortest and ending with the tallest, first take turns to throw darts at the board with their 'wrong' hands. This is their right hand if they are left-handed, their left hand if they are right-handed. Ambidextrous players thus enjoy a small initial advantage. Eventually, each Punter will hit one of the twenty numbers on the board. This becomes the Punter's Private Number. Any Punter who hits the Private Number of another Punter during this wrong-handed and admittedly somewhat dangerous dart-throwing bonanza must try again, and again, and just keep on trying until she manages to hit an unclaimed number.

3. Moving in sequence, once more beginning with the shortest, Punters now take turns to throw three darts at the board. Their objective is to become 'Killers' and to do this they must hit their own Private Number nine times, giving them nine lives. (Inept

darts players may by mutual agreement reduce the number of lives needed to become a Killer.) Hitting the main body of their Private Number gives them one life. Hitting the double ring of their Private Number gives them two lives; hitting the treble ring gives them three lives; hitting the outer bull's eye gives them four lives, while the inner bull's eye gives them five lives.

4. If one Punter hits another Punter's Private Number, then the lucky 'victim' gains another life. If a Punter hits a Killer's Private Number (see below), then the errant Punter loses a life.

5. A player who gets nine or more lives becomes a Killer. If the Punter scores more than one life *with the dart which makes her a Killer*, then these extra lives are added to her total as Life Insurance. Thus a Killer may have anywhere between nine and thirteen lives. (The latter—which is the strongest position a Killer can be in— happens if an eight-lived Punter hits the inner bull's eye and becomes a Killer by scoring five more lives.)

6. Killers take their turn to throw darts in the normal sequence of players. The objective of a Killer is to kill all other players by hitting their Private Numbers as many times as it takes to do this. A Killer takes one life from *any* player, Punter or Killer, *including herself*, when she hits the main body of their Private Number, two lives when she hits the double ring, and three lives when she hits the treble ring.

7. Any Killer who falls below nine lives becomes a Punter Once Again.

8. The winner is the player with the most lives when the time-limit expires, or the only player left in the game if every other player has been killed before the time-limit expires.

9. If there is a tie for the winning position, then all *losing* players, beginning as always with the shortest, throw three darts at the board. The winner of the tie is the player whose Private Number is hit the *fewest* times during this Revenge of the Punters (with the double ring counting two lives, and the treble ring counting three, as always).

HOW TO WIN KILLER

You will do much better at Killer if you can throw darts accurately, there can be no doubt about this. If you are so bad at darts that you are glad just to hit the board, and have no control to speak of over where on the board any particular dart lands, then you will do very badly at Killer. Those of your darts that do hit the board will land, effectively, at random. This means that, until you become a Killer, which seems a most unlikely eventuality, you will help every other player by giving each one a life for every life that you give yourself. If they can control their darts better than you, then they will become Killers before you do and you will be in deep, deep trouble. If none of the players can control the darts, of course, then you will not be at a particular disadvantage, but really you might as well all go off and play a game of Banging Our Heads Against a Brick Wall as try playing Killer.

Assuming, therefore, that you can control the darts somewhat, the first part of the game is not really very strategic. Pretty much the best thing to do is to try as hard as you can to become the first Killer on the block by throwing as accurately as you can at your own Private Number. Professional players will ignore the big scores coming from the bull's eyes, since just a little mistake risks handing extra lives as a free gift to rivals. The cool cats will just try and hit as may of their own Private Trebles as they can.

As soon as one player has become a Killer, of course, the game is transformed, and indeed it might well be transformed in anticipation of this happening. A lone Killer's strategy is pretty straightforward. She wants to stop other Punters becoming Killers, so she will attack those Punters with the most lives. This strategy will, however, be qualified by the actual scatter of Private Numbers around the board, since only a super-cool Killer will go after Punters whose Private Numbers sit next to her own on the board— the costs of a slight misfire are just too great. So Killers will go for high-scoring Punters, especially those with private Numbers far from their own.

The Punters, faced with a lone Killer, face a more agonizing strategic dilemma, however. One solution is for each Punter to continue with her own frantic dash for those extra lives that will make her a Killer too. An alternative strategy is for some or all of the Punters to form a coalition, with the intention of giving as many lives as fast as possible to just one of their number, presumably the one who currently has the most lives. The aim is to turn this person into a Killer Number Two with the job of taking out Killer Number

One in a hail of darts thrown in the interests of the coalition as a whole. Once more, the scatter of Private Numbers around the board may suggest the most sensible coalitions. Players with adjacent Private Numbers make obvious coalition partners, since a player who fails to hit the number she is aiming for may still give a life to some other coalition member.

The problem of course is that there is no guarantee that Killer Number Two won't turn on the very people who made her what she is—after all, none of the other Punters can kill a Killer. The coalition risks creating a monster that they just can't control yet, if they don't create a second Killer as fast as possible, then they will all be picked-off at leisure by the lone Killer, who will have nothing at all to fear. Again, the precise location of Private Numbers on the board may come to the coalition's rescue. Three players with adjacent numbers may decide to make the middle player a Killer, in the knowledge that she may be loath to attack them once the deed has been done, for fear of hitting her own Private Number and thereby shooting herself painfully in the foot.

The bottom line in all of this, which not all players realize but which you would do very well to remember, is that only a Killer can kill a Killer. This means that, once there is one Killer in the game there will always be a Killer in the game, unless a lone Killer mistakenly hits her own Private Number and self-destructs. If possible, therefore, and if there are enough players, the Coalition of Punters is actually better trying to create at least *two* new Killers, setting up a triangular war among the Killers that might serve to divert attention from less well-endowed members of the game.

Ultimately, the game will almost certainly resolve into a war among the Killers. Players, even bad players, *will* keep scoring lives until at least one of them becomes a Killer. Unless the lone first Killer can destroy all Punters before they have a chance to regroup, other Killers may well be created. It might on the face of things seem that Killers will then have to balance the desire to attack other Killers—in order to create a free fire killing zone in which they can massacre the poor Punters—against the desire to attack defenceless Punters in the knowledge that the game can only finally be won by killing Punters.

On thinking about it, however, smart Killers will realize that, as long as there is another Killer in the game, their precious darts are wasted on killing Punters. This is because each Punter-death helps *rival* Killers as much as it helps the Killer throwing the fatal dart. Once there is more than one Killer in the game, therefore, the most effective place for any Killer's dart is in the heart of a rival Killer.

The game will finally be won by a Killer who can achieve a position as lone Killer and then use dart-throwing skills to keep at bay those Punters who are on the verge of Killer status, while slowly but surely whittling away the lives of the other Punters. The trouble is that, except for the very finest of darts players, this is an almost impossibly tall order, provided the Punters are able to organize, along the lines suggested above, to create a rival Killer whom they hope will protect their interests. Thus the essential political puzzle in this game has to do with the need to protect yourself from exploitation and tyranny by creating someone who will, by virtue of being able to protect you, also have the power to exploit and tyrannize you should she choose to do so. Such, of course, is life.

13 So?

Games are games and politics is, of course, politics. Many readers will no doubt be appalled at my apparently flippant equation of the two. However, as I said at the beginning of this book, these games are not about the great issues of politics. They are about the means to achieve such ends. In the real world, as any philosopher will tell you, it is quite impossible to separate means from ends in such a simple-minded way. Many horrible things have been done in the name of great and noble causes and some of these low means have obviously distorted, even confounded, the lofty ends involved.

Mere mortals, however, cannot study everything at once. One of the ways in which we try to come to grips with a difficult and complicated world is to draw distinctions that we know very well to be arbitrary and unrealistic in the hope that, by holding a number of things constant, we can gain at least some intellectual purchase on the others.

This is one justification for the cynical and amoral tenor of this book. Ethics and ideals have been steadfastly ignored, even ridiculed, in an attempt to prize open the Pandora's box of political strategy. 'Good' politicians, after all, may well be good, but they are also politicians. Politics is about power. Power is about getting your own way, whatever that might be. I do, therefore, leave the sermons to those better-equipped to deliver them.

This book is, however, very easy for you to pass judgement on since, above all else, games should be fun to play. If you did not enjoy playing these games even a little bit, then the book has failed, that at least is quite clear. The proof of this particular pudding really is in the eating.

There are lots of games around, however, so why should you waste your time playing these when you could be having lots of fun, and maybe even making some money, playing One-Eyed Jack or Kansas City Low Ball? The answer is that, when we start thinking about politics, games and the real world actually do come quite close together.

161

Games, as we have just seen, are about means and nothing else since the goals that the players must achieve are almost always arbitrary and irrelevant. Talk to any soccer fanatic about how kicking a ball into a net doesn't actually have anything to do with the complex and important problems that human beings have to grapple with in their 'real' lives and, if you are not assaulted on the spot, you will be given directions to the nearest mental hospital.

The fact that the goals in a game are arbitrary, however, is not the point. A game is a particular type of conflict between a group of calculating and motivated players. It presents a particular social puzzle, a particular structure of human interaction. These interactions are not only fascinating in their own right but, at a slightly more abstract level, can be seen as patterns that recur over and over again in the social world. This means that games can be used as shorthand descriptions of particular types of social interaction. A good game, in these terms, describes a rich and intriguing social interaction that can be found in a range of different and important areas of the social life we all love to live.

Thus poker, when all is said and done, *is* just poker. But we can gain deep insights into other social interactions by talking about them *as if* the participants were in fact playing poker. Any showdown between highly rational people when each has different strengths, when each must make moves without fully revealing these strengths to others, and when each is trying to work out whether or not the others might be bluffing about what they've got, is a little bit like poker. It does therefore make sense to think of aspects of a strike, a hijacking, a kidnapping, or an international stand-off such as the Cuban Missile Crisis *as if* the actors were playing poker. To take another example, at least one author has produced an interesting and provocative study of guerrilla warfare, of which Mao Zedong was a master, by likening it to Go, the ancient Chinese game of encirclement.

Given the way in which good game-players are forced to think, not only about their own moves, but about how their opponents might react to these moves, and how they in turn might react to their opponents' reactions, it is no accident that the language of games forms part of the language of politics, with its gambles and its gambits, its bids and its bluffs, its races, its rounds and its lotteries. People can become fascinated with politics for the same reason that they can become fascinated with games. Both are more or less stylized mechanisms for achieving a certain set of objectives with a limited set of resources, when others are trying to do precisely the same thing.

There is even a theory of games, game theory, much of which sits in a somewhat uneasy relationship to the games that you have, I hope, just been playing. Game theory is self-consciously rigid and formal, as of course it must be in order to bring rigorous logical tools to bear upon the social interactions that it models. The games in this book deal with essentially the same interactions, but are self-consciously loose and informal, setting out to stir gut feelings rather than solve formal problems. One book that will allow readers to peel up a corner on game theory, however does manage to bridge the almost unbridgeable gap between the accurate statement of rigorous logic on one hand and the lively presentation of real social interactions on the other. This is Dixit and Nalebuff's, *Thinking Strategically*, the book that is probably the best next thing to read for any innocent bystander whose appetite for something a little more meaty has been triggered by playing political games.

Many of the basic ideas of game theory do help us to think about down and dirty political games in a more productive manner. One of these is the standard classification of games into three basic types: games of pure co-operation, games of pure conflict, and games that are a mixture of the two.

In games of pure conflict—often described as 'zero sum' games but more accurately known as 'constant sum' games—everything that is won by any of the players must be forgone by the others. If two people play, then everything I win leaves that much less for you. Everything I lose leaves that much more for you. A very large number of gambling games, spectator sports, and games played simply for fun fall into this category. Examples include poker, chess, soccer, boxing, and baseball. In the real world, needless to say, things are rarely so clear-cut. There are, however, some real political games of pure conflict, including presidential elections and some wars (although not nuclear war, which everyone can lose).

More often than not in real-life games, however, some of the outcomes make two or more people better off at the same time. Such people obviously have an incentive to co-operate with each other so as to achieve these outcomes.

Games of *pure* co-operation, which are at the other end of the spectrum from games of pure conflict, are even more rare in the real world than games of pure conflict. Even on those few occasions when everyone wants precisely the same thing, however, communication blockages can sometimes make co-operation difficult to achieve. A gaming example of this is charades, in which everyone tries to guess the charade while at the same time the person acting out the charade is trying to help them, and there are no real 'winners' or 'losers' except the groups of players as a whole. Everyone wins or everyone loses, and charades is only a game at all because the person acting the charade is not allowed to speak. If she is allowed to tell you what the charade is about, then the game loses its point entirely.

A real-life co-operation game arises if you become separated from a dear friend in a busy shopping area. You really do want to find each other, but cannot communicate. You are in effect playing a game that we might think of as 'Rendezvous'. To 'win' it, each player must meet the other and to do this each must try to work out what the other will do, what they think the other person thinks that they will do, and so on:

> Jack wants to meet Jill
>
> Jill wants to meet Jack
> > but neither of them knows where
>
> Jack knows that Jill wants to meet Jack
> > and knows that Jill knows that he knows this
>
> Jill knows that Jack wants to meet Jill
> > and knows that Jack knows that she knows this
> > > but neither of them knows where
>
> Jack decides to meet Jill where Jill would decide to meet Jack
>
> Jill decides to meet Jack where Jack would decide to meet Jill
>
> They meet, or not, as the case may be
> > and no matter how much each one loves the other
> > > it makes no difference

This game would disappear completely if both Jack and Jill had mobile phones since, unless they have decided to play

Hide and Seek rather than Rendezvous, no conflict at all is involved.

Real-world examples of co-operation games include generals trying to unite their armies under radio silence, civil servants trying to give the same answers to an investigative committee, or criminals trying to produce the same alibi under police questioning. In each case the essential strategic logic involves thinking 'what will she think that I think that she thinks that I think . . . is the right thing to do?' In practice, games like this are often resolved with reasonable success because the real world is full of clues—favourite pubs, favourite colours, high hills, and low valleys—that can help people solve co-operation games. Even with the best will in the world, however, and with the most earnest desire to co-operate, communication problems can mean that they don't always succeed.

Most real-life games, and certainly most political games, involve a mixture of conflict and co-operation. This combination defines the final category of games, which are usually referred to as 'mixed motive' or 'variable-sum' games. Gaming examples of mixed-motive games are rather rare since most people seem to prefer clear-cut winners and losers when they play games for fun. Team games, however, can often produce mixed motives within the team, even if not in the game as a whole. An individual player wants the team to win, of course, but also wants to do well personally. Thus a team of long-distance runners or cyclists must pace each other; if they don't, their team will stand no chance of winning. But each will also want to beat the other members of the team when it comes to the final sprint. At the start of the race, there is almost pure co-operation; at the finish it is almost pure conflict. Somewhere in between the start and the finish there is a mixture of the two.

The Selfish Footballer is also playing a mixed-motive game, wanting her team to win, of course, but wanting to get all the goals herself. The crunch comes when she must decide whether to pass the ball to someone with a better chance of scoring, or to press on herself with a solo run. The team does better, on the balance of probabilities, if she passes, but she might do better if she hogs the ball.

Political examples of mixed-motive games are legion; most of politics consists of balancing mixed motives. One graphic example from the bad old days of the Cold War should illustrate this point. Two heads of State are contemplating waging nuclear war on each other. Each would most of all like to beat the other and rule the world. This gives each an incentive to launch a pre-emptive strike against the other. If the strike is launched, however, the other side might retaliate seconds before being obliterated and the ensuing nuclear holocaust would make both worse off than they were before they started. Each therefore has an incentive to co-operate with the other to avoid the destruction of the world since, if they fail, there will be no world to rule. Both motives operate simultaneously, pulling the politicians making the decisions in different directions.

What is especially relevant about this example is that game theorists on both sides modelled the apocalyptic real world possibilities as games, and wrote things that were indeed read by the people advising those with their fingers on the real triggers. For an outstanding example of this type of analysis, written at the very height of the Cold War, see Thomas Schelling's *Strategy of Conflict*. (And for other stimulating game models of real human interactions, don't miss the same author's *Micromotives and Macrobehaviour*.)

The games in this book are mixed-motive games for most of their duration. Towards the end of the games, conflict tends to assert itself however, since there is after all only one winner. Until this point has been reached, the games are designed so that no player can stand much of a chance of winning without engaging in some form of co-operation with others.

While the games in this book can be categorized in this general way, using some of the general terms used by game theorists, they are too loosely specified to be analysed mathematically in any rigorous manner. Too little is known about what the other players have got by way of resources or what they want by way of outcomes. There are too many variables, there is too little time, the rules are too vague in many places, and there is that incessant pounding rock music. . . . All of this is quite deliberate. The general set-up of the games is designed to force people to make mistakes by putting them under pressure; to leave them at least partially in the dark about what, precisely is going on; to encourage cheating; and, time after time, to confront players suddenly with the unexpected social shocks that human interactions always generate.

Game theorists talk about these things in terms of 'imperfect' and 'incomplete' information and then set out to model these in a rigorous manner, in what has become one of the most difficult and technical branches of game theory. Rather than try and stuff these crucial features of real human interactions back in the box, however, the games in this book let them all hang out in an untidy but, I hope, essentially more realistic manner.

One of the paradoxes of game theory, indeed, is that, just as it begins to get more realistic by taking on board some of the more interesting complexities of actual human interactions, its fundamental reliance upon rigorous logical argument as a way of doing things causes it to seize up and become impossibly dense and complicated. There is an annoying tendency of game-theoretic discussions to be consumed by their own rigour just as they are getting interesting!

One of the seductive aspects of actually playing games, in contrast, is that we can start with a very simple set of written rules and set the games in motion. We can then observe the ways in which these rules interact to generate a complex web of human interaction. Not only can be seen how a rich social complexity can result from the interaction of a simple set of rules, but we can play with the rules to see how apparently small changes in these can sometimes have big social effects.

There is, as there always is, alas, a price to pay for all of this. Game theory does have its rigorous system of logic as at least one tool for separating the good, the bad, and the ugly among discussions of games. The alternative that I am promoting here—which involves setting games in motion and then watching all of the marvellous social complexity that can be generated by a simple set of rules—is more an aesthetic experience than a logical one. That doesn't bother me, but I have found on my travels that it does bother some people.

None of this makes for neat conclusions, of course, which is why I do not offer any. Play the games.

References

Dixit, Avinash, and Barry Nalebuff, *Thinking Strategically* (New York: W. W. Norton, 1991)

Downs, Anthony, *An Economic Theory of Democracy* (New York: Harper & Row, 1957)

Hardin, Russell, *Collective Action* (Baltimore: Johns Hopkins University Press, 1982)

Laing, R. D., *Knots* (Harmondsworth: Penguin Books, 1972)

Laver, Michael, *Private Desires, Political Action* (London: Sage Publications, 1997)

—— and Norman Schofield, *Multiparty Government* (Oxford: Oxford University Press, 1990)

Olson, Mancur, *The Logic of Collective Action* (Cambridge, Mass.: Harvard University Press, 1965)

Ostrom, Elinor, *Governing the Commons* (New York: Cambridge University Press, 1990)

Riker, William, *The Theory of Political Coalitions* (New Haven: Yale University Press, 1962)

Schelling, Thomas, *Strategy of Conflict* (Cambridge, Mass.: Harvard University Press, 1960)

—— *Micromotives and Macrobehaviour* (New York: W. W. Norton, 1978)

Shepsle, Kenneth A., and Stephen Bonchek, *Analysing Politics* (New York: W. W. Norton, 1997)

Taylor, Michael, *Community, Anarchy and Liberty* (Cambridge: Cambridge University Press, 1982)

Ware, Alan, *Political Parties and Party Systems* (Oxford: Oxford University Press, 1996)

Index

Index

Index

Index

OXFORD

MORE OXFORD PAPERBACKS

This book is just one of nearly 1000 Oxford Paperbacks currently in print. If you would like details of other Oxford Paperbacks, including titles in the World's Classics, Oxford Reference, Oxford Books, OPUS, Past Masters, Oxford Authors, and Oxford Shakespeare series, please write to:

UK and Europe: Oxford Paperbacks Publicity Manager, Arts and Reference Publicity Department, Oxford University Press, Walton Street, Oxford OX2 6DP.

Customers in UK and Europe will find Oxford Paperbacks available in all good bookshops. But in case of difficulty please send orders to the Cash-with-Order Department, Oxford University Press Distribution Services, Saxon Way West, Corby, Northants NN18 9ES. Tel: 01536 741519; Fax: 01536 746337. Please send a cheque for the total cost of the books, plus £1.75 postage and packing for orders under £20; £2.75 for orders over £20. Customers outside the UK should add 10% of the cost of the books for postage and packing.

USA: Oxford Paperbacks Marketing Manager, Oxford University Press, Inc., 200 Madison Avenue, New York, N.Y. 10016.

Canada: Trade Department, Oxford University Press, 70 Wynford Drive, Don Mills, Ontario M3C 1J9.

Australia: Trade Marketing Manager, Oxford University Press, G.P.O. Box 2784Y, Melbourne 3001, Victoria.

South Africa: Oxford University Press, P.O. Box 1141, Cape Town 8000.

POLITICS IN OXFORD PAPERBACKS
GOD SAVE ULSTER!

The Religion and Politics of Paisleyism

Steve Bruce

Ian Paisley is the only modern Western leader to have founded his own Church and political party, and his enduring popularity and success mirror the complicated issues which continue to plague Northern Ireland. This book is the first serious analysis of his religious and political careers and a unique insight into Unionist politics and religion in Northern Ireland today.

Since it was founded in 1951, the Free Presbyterian Church of Ulster has grown steadily; it now comprises some 14,000 members in fifty congregations in Ulster and ten branches overseas. The Democratic Unionist Party, formed in 1971, now speaks for about half of the Unionist voters in Northern Ireland, and the personal standing of the man who leads both these movements was confirmed in 1979 when Ian R. K. Paisley received more votes than any other member of the European Parliament. While not neglecting Paisley's 'charismatic' qualities, Steve Bruce argues that the key to his success has been his ability to embody and represent traditional evangelical Protestantism and traditional Ulster Unionism.

'original and profound . . . I cannot praise this book too highly.' Bernard Crick, *New Society*

POPULAR SCIENCE FROM OXFORD PAPERBACKS

THE SELFISH GENE

Second Edition

Richard Dawkins

Our genes made us. We animals exist for their preservation and are nothing more than their throwaway survival machines. The world of the selfish gene is one of savage competition, ruthless exploitation, and deceit. But what of the acts of apparent altruism found in nature—the bees who commit suicide when they sting to protect the hive, or the birds who risk their lives to warn the flock of an approaching hawk? Do they contravene the fundamental law of gene selfishness? By no means: Dawkins shows that the selfish gene is also the subtle gene. And he holds out the hope that our species—alone on earth—has the power to rebel against the designs of the selfish gene. This book is a call to arms. It is both manual and manifesto, and it grips like a thriller.

The Selfish Gene, Richard Dawkins's brilliant first book and still his most famous, is an international bestseller in thirteen languages. For this greatly expanded edition, endnotes have been added, giving fascinating reflections on the original text, and there are two major new chapters.

'learned, witty, and very well written . . . exhilaratingly good.' Sir Peter Medawar, *Spectator*

'Who should read this book? Everyone interested in the universe and their place in it.' Jeffrey R. Baylis, *Animal Behaviour*

'the sort of popular science writing that makes the reader feel like a genius' *New York Times*

HISTORY IN OXFORD PAPERBACKS

THE STRUGGLE FOR
THE MASTERY OF EUROPE 1848–1918

A. J. P. Taylor

The fall of Metternich in the revolutions of 1848 heralded an era of unprecedented nationalism in Europe, culminating in the collapse of the Hapsburg, Romanov, and Hohenzollern dynasties at the end of the First World War. In the intervening seventy years the boundaries of Europe changed dramatically from those established at Vienna in 1815. Cavour championed the cause of *Risorgimento* in Italy; Bismarck's three wars brought about the unification of Germany; Serbia and Bulgaria gained their independence courtesy of the decline of Turkey—'the sick man of Europe'; while the great powers scrambled for places in the sun in Africa. However, with America's entry into the war and President Wilson's adherence to idealistic internationalist principles, Europe ceased to be the centre of the world, although its problems, still primarily revolving around nationalist aspirations, were to smash the Treaty of Versailles and plunge the world into war once more.

A. J. P. Taylor has drawn the material for his account of this turbulent period from the many volumes of diplomatic documents which have been published in the five major European languages. By using vivid language and forceful characterization, he has produced a book that is as much a work of literature as a contribution to scientific history.

'One of the glories of twentieth-century writing.'
Observer

Oxford
Paperback
Reference

OXFORD PAPERBACK REFERENCE

From *Art and Artists* to *Zoology*, the Oxford Paperback Reference series offers the very best subject reference books at the most affordable prices.

Authoritative, accessible, and up to date, the series features dictionaries in key student areas, as well as a range of fascinating books for a general readership. Included are such well-established titles as Fowler's *Modern English Usage*, Margaret Drabble's *Concise Companion to English Literature*, and the bestselling science and medical dictionaries.

The series has now been relaunched in handsome new covers. Highlights include new editions of some of the most popular titles, as well as brand new paperback reference books on *Politics*, *Philosophy*, and *Twentieth-Century Poetry*.

With new titles being constantly added, and existing titles regularly updated, Oxford Paperback Reference is unrivalled in its breadth of coverage and expansive publishing programme. New dictionaries of *Film*, *Economics*, *Linguistics*, *Architecture*, *Archaeology*, *Astronomy*, and *The Bible* are just a few of those coming in the future.

Oxford
Paperback
Reference

THE OXFORD DICTIONARY OF PHILOSOPHY

Edited by Simon Blackburn

* 2,500 entries covering the entire span of the subject including the most recent terms and concepts

* Biographical entries for nearly 500 philosophers

* Chronology of philosophical events

From Aristotle to Zen, this is the most comprehensive, authoritative, and up to date dictionary of philosophy available. Ideal for students or a general readership, it provides lively and accessible coverage of not only the Western philosophical tradition but also important themes from Chinese, Indian, Islamic, and Jewish philosophy. The paperback includes a new Chronology.

'an excellent source book and can be strongly recommended . . . there are generous and informative entries on the great philosophers . . . Overall the entries are written in an informed and judicious manner.'
Times Higher Education Supplement

Oxford
Paperback
Reference

THE CONCISE OXFORD DICTIONARY OF POLITICS

Edited by Iain McLean

Written by an expert team of political scientists from Warwick University, this is the most authoritative and up-to-date dictionary of politics available.

* Over 1,500 entries provide truly international coverage of major political institutions, thinkers and concepts

* From Western to Chinese and Muslim political thought

* Covers new and thriving branches of the subject, including international political economy, voting theory, and feminism

* Appendix of political leaders

* Clear, no-nonsense definitions of terms such as veto and subsidiarity

OPUS

TWENTIETH-CENTURY FRENCH PHILOSOPHY

Eric Matthews

This book gives a chronological survey of the works of the major French philosophers of the twentieth century.

Eric Matthews offers various explanations for the enduring importance of philosophy in French intellectual life and traces the developments which French philosophy has taken in the twentieth century from its roots in the thought of Descartes, with examinations of key figures such as Bergson, Sartre, Marcel, Merleau-Ponty, Foucault, and Derrida, and the recent French Feminists.

'*Twentieth-Century French Philosophy* is a clear, yet critical introduction to contemporary French Philosophy. . . . The undergraduate or other reader who comes to the area for the first time will gain a definite sense of an intellectual movement with its own questions and answers and its own rigour . . . not least of the book's virtues is its clarity.'
Garrett Barden
Author of *After Principles*

OXFORD

FOUR ESSAYS ON LIBERTY

Isaiah Berlin

'those who value liberty for its own sake believe that
to be free to choose, and not to be chosen for, is an
inalienable ingredient in what makes human beings
human'
Introduction to *Four Essays On Liberty*

Political Ideas in the Twentieth Century
Historical Inevitability
Two Concepts of Liberty
John Stuart Mill and the Ends of Life

These four essays deal with the various aspects of
individual liberty, including the distinction between
positive and negative liberty and the necessity of
rejecting determinism if we wish to keep hold of the
notions of human responsibility and freedom.

'practically every paragraph introduces us to half a
dozen new ideas and as many thinkers—the landscape flashes past, peopled with familiar and unfamiliar people, all arguing incessantly'
New Society

A Very Short Introduction

POLITICS

Kenneth Minogue

Since politics is both complex and controversial it is easy to miss the wood for the trees. In this Very Short Introduction Kenneth Minogue has brought the many dimensions of politics into a single focus: he discusses both the everyday grind of democracy and the attraction of grand ideals such as freedom and justice.

'Kenneth Minogue is a very lively stylist who does not distort difficult ideas.'
Maurice Cranston

'a dazzling but unpretentious display of great scholarship and humane reflection'
Professor Neil O'Sullivan, University of Hull

'Minogue is an admirable choice for showing us the nuts and bolts of the subject.'
Nicholas Lezard, *Guardian*

'This is a fascinating book which sketches, in a very short space, one view of the nature of politics . . . the reader is challenged, provoked and stimulated by Minogue's trenchant views.'
Talking Politics